Marketing
And Branding

The art of developing and managing brands

Eugênio Bispo Melo
Brand Manager

Editorial coordination: LivroEbook Diagramação e Design
Translation: Google translate
Grammar review: Eugênio Bispo Melo
Cover: LivroEbook Diagramação e Design

Melo, Eugênio Bispo
Marketing and Branding – The art of developing and managing brands / Eugênio Bispo Melo. LivroEbook, 2024.

ISBN: 978-65-01-20208-2
I. Marketing II. Branding III. Gestão de marcas.

SYNOPSIS

In its global edition, the book brings the main marketing concepts, together with the most important and innovative aspects of brand management in Brazil and worldwide. It brings to light the importance of service in chain stores, franchises, dealerships, supermarkets, delivery, as well as the astronomical growth of the digital platform in the global market. It shows how the brand's image and positioning have been flexible in the face of changes in the economy and in consumer buying behavior, as well as a preface by the father of brand positioning, *Al Ries*. A surprising and unique book in the publishing market that brings together methods, concepts and practices and, therefore, can be considered a parameter in the academic and governmental environment. Written by the marketing and branding specialist, this book reflects the urgent need to apply new concepts and resources related to brand management in the corporate and government market.

About The Author

Eugênio Bispo is a writer, consultant, speaker and director of Global Consultoria (*Marketing & Branding Consulting*). He has a degree in tourism, a postgraduate degree in business management, a postgraduate degree in communication and marketing and an MBA in quality management. He has written several articles on brand management published on websites specializing in economics, marketing and business. He developed the remarkable professional qualification and classification program (*Global Professional Service*), which also covers technology services (digital platform). He developed several methods, concepts and practices related to marketing and brand management, including the concept of *Government Branding*, in addition to stimulating the image and positioning of the brand in Brazil and in the world (*Brazil Branding Group*). He began his career effectively in 2011 developing academic research and consulting. He is an expert in customer service and a reference in brand management and strategic marketing planning. He is also a project management and quality analyst (GPE, PEP & EIP).

Pioneer in the art of developing and managing brands!
Contact: eugeniobispomelo@gmail.com

DEDICATION:

I dedicate this book to the memory of my father, **Eugênio de Freitas Melo**, whom I thank for his total dedication to my academic education.

IN MEMORY

RECOGNITION:

Thanks to the father of positioning, *AL RIES,* for his memorable preface and dedication to my book.

PRESENTATION

Quality is the best tool to correctly position any product, service or brand in the consumer's mind!

Eugênio Bispo Melo

This book shows the relationship between brand positioning and satisfying market needs and desires. Therefore, the idea was to develop concepts, methods and practices that refer us to market management, but with an emphasis on brand image and governance. In this way, marketing collaborates perfectly with the idea that it is not possible to satisfy needs and desires without the brand assuming a prominent position in the face of competition and global competitiveness.

Thus, in its global edition, this book fills an extremely important gap, due to the lack of a bibliography concerning the subject covered in Brazil and in the world. In other words, it is an book that elucidates, demystifies and heals the importance of brand management in modern marketing. Breaking paradigms or mistaken thoughts about brand management. Considered a parameter in academic, corporate and governmental circles, this book reflects the urgent importance of changes in the way of managing brands in Brazil and in the world. Each chapter is responsible for the longevity and maintenance of the brand, whose main objective is to define marketing strategies, as well as the brand positioning in the consumer's mind.

An amazing book that provokes a deep reflection on the way we act and think in relation to products, services and brands. On the other hand, this book contributes to economic, social and environmental development, as the brand is closely related to improving the quality of life and self-esteem. The author has developed innovative methods, practices and concepts that help us to gain a better understanding of the topic, considering that the brand is an extremely important indicator of trust and credibility in the market. The work also shows in a very clear and objective way, why the satisfaction of needs, desires and expectations exert a direct influence on the consumer's purchasing behavior. However, this book addresses important aspects of our lives and that are rooted in the brand's behavior and relationship with the consumer.

Keywords: Marketing, Branding, Relationship, Behavior, Entertainment, Governance, Competitiveness, Transformation, Quality, Product, Service, Technology and Commoditization.

PREFACE

In the spring of 1972, Jack Trout and I wrote a series of articles for a marketing publication called Advertising Age. The title is called "The Positioning Era Cometh."

Advertising Age articles aroused a great deal of interest in advertising and marketing in America, but this interest has not spread around the world considering that all of our examples are from American companies and brands. However, in the fall of 1972 I was surprised to be invited to Brazil to give a series of lectures on the concept of positioning. In less than six months, this concept had traveled 4,773 miles from New York to São Paulo.

So I went to Brazil to participate in three days of meetings with executives in the advertising area, my first trip outside the United States in order to talk about the concept of positioning. Since then, I have made several trips to Brazil to give lectures on positioning and other marketing concepts. I have traveled to Brazil more than any other country! This is because of the intense interest in advertising and marketing in Brazil.

Since 1972 there have been many other developments in Marketing, Branding and Positioning. The author, Eugênio Bispo, covered all these developments in his book, “MARKETING and BRANDING - The art of developing and managing brands”. I'm not surprised that a Brazilian writer has written such a comprehensive and innovative book on the subject in Brazil and around the world. Since my first trip to São Paulo in 1972, I have made several other trips addressing this topic in more than 60 countries, including Saudi Arabia, Russia, Turkey, Nigeria, Malaysia, China, Japan, Australia, Philippines, Singapore, Sri Lanka among others, but none of these countries impressed me with their advertising, marketing and knowledge as much as the people in Brazil.

So, I wasn't surprised that a Brazilian writer had the knowledge to write such a comprehensive and innovative book about the image and positioning of brands in Brazil and in the world.

Marketing is not an easy discipline to master! However, there is a myth among people and marketers that marketing is just advertising. This is the biggest problem faced in advertising and marketing.

Marketing is not just marketing, it is also the most difficult business technique to master. In addition, marketing is a discipline that is constantly changing, depending on the consumer's choice and behavior process.

Then there's the great media revolution, with the Internet dramatically changing the way companies spend their resources on advertising and marketing.

We also have the consumer revolution, with many buyers looking for brands that are socially responsible. How to master a discipline as difficult as marketing? A good place to start is, without a doubt, by reading Eugênio Bispo book.

Again, I would suggest.

Al Ries, President of Ries & Ries, Marketing Consulting.

SUMMARY

DEDICATION: 5

RECOGNITION:..7

PRESENTATION 9

Preface...11

Introduction...17

Chapter I..19
Brand Planning and Development 19

PRODUCT LINE EXTENSION..23

BRAND NAME STRATEGIES 24

PORTFOLIO ANALYSIS 25

BRAND EQUITY 27

CO-BRANDING..29

PRODUCT LIFE CYCLE ANALYSIS 29

ANALYSIS OF GROWTH OPPORTUNITIES IN THE MARKET 33

MARKETING COMMUNICATION 41

COMMUNICATION PROCESS 43

DEVELOPMENT OF MARKETING COMMUNICATION 44

SELECTION OF COMMUNICATION CHANNELS 46

Chapter 2 48
STRATEGIC MARKETING PLANNING.......................................48

MARKETING AND CONCEPTS..49

WHO IS MARKETING INTENDED FOR 49

HOW MARKETING IS CHANGING..50

MARKETING ORIENTATION FOR THE MARKET 52

MARKETING PLAN....53
CORPORATE STRATEGIC PLANNING....53
COMPETITION ANALYSIS....56
GENERAL THEORY OF SYSTEMS....59
COMPONENTS AND CHARACTERISTICS OF A SYSTEM....60
TOTAL QUALITY....62
PRINCIPLES OF TOTAL QUALITY....62
THEORY OF HUMAN NEEDS....64
LEADERSHIP IN ORGANIZATIONS....66
POWER AND LEADERSHIP....67

Chapter 3....69
Branding Service....69
INTANGIBILITY SCALE....77
SERVICE QUALITY MANAGEMENT....80
SERVICE MANAGEMENT MODEL....82
POSITIONING AND IMAGE OF THE SERVICE BRAND....83
DISTRIBUTION OF SERVICES....85
SERVICE LOGISTICS....86
CUSTOMER RELATIONSHIP MANAGEMENT (CRM)....90
FORMS OF COMMUNICATION IN SERVICES....91
PROFESSIONAL ETHIC....92

Chapter 4....94
Brand Visual Communication....94
COMMUNICATION WITH THE BRAND....97

Chapter 5....99
Brand Values and Beliefs....99

Chapter 6....102
Brand Evolution....102

Chapter 7 105
Crisis Management and Brand Revitalization 105

Chapter 8 108
Brand Strategic Planning 108

Chapter 9 117
The practice of branding on social media 117

Chapter 10 120
The Practice of Branding in Communication 120

Chapter 11 125
Building Brands and Relationships 125

Chapter 12 131
Marketing Before and After Branding 131

Chapter 13 138
Government Branding...138

Chapter 14 140
Virtual Brand Management...140

Chapter 15 143
Multifunctional Marketing 143

Case study **146**
Bibliographic reference: 148

INTRODUCTION

The brand was for a long time the introduction of the product or service. Today there is a clear notion that the brand means much more than its simple identification. However, over the years, the brand has become something more flexible and tangible, as it reflects the perceptions of the final consumer. The brand then moved to a denser stage of human thought. Now it is not just the name, term or symbol, but everything that the brand represents. That way, we hardly forget something that can satisfy our needs, desires and expectations. In this sense, everything we learn throughout life is extremely significant. The human mind records the most important moments of our life. Fixes in memory everything we live (past, present and future). Therefore, the purchase decision is just as important as the choice of brand.

In the manufacturing industry, the brand plays a fundamental role, as we need to know which brand to trust. The brand's goal is to reduce complexity about the product or service. In other words, this means that in the manufacturing industry the brand is the only indicator of trust and credibility. On the other hand, in the services sector, the brand has a more humanitarian and charismatic role, because of its involvement with the human element. In this way, the brand is no longer synonymous with credibility and temporarily acts as a supporting role. As the service meets the needs, desires and expectations of the consumer, the brand assumes a prominent and competitive position in relation to the competition.

So, the service needs professional qualification, as it is not possible to offer a good service without the effective participation of the human element. For this reason, the quality of service has a direct influence on brand positioning. But, after all, why is brand management so important? To answer this question, just look at the number of brands that have registered losses in recent years. Famous brands, however, record losses and layoffs!

It is important to remember that any brand has a direct and personal involvement with the product or service. However, what characterizes consumer loyalty is the transparency with which the product or service is offered to the market. This concept takes us to both the corporate and government markets. In the near future, we will have smarter brands due to technology and global competitiveness. This also means that we will have more transparent brands that are aware of their social role in relation to the consumer. In this way, the brand definitively synthesizes the way in which marketing meets the needs, desires and expectations of contemporary society.

CHAPTER I

BRAND PLANNING AND DEVELOPMENT

Let's start by talking about three important elements in the positioning of any brand: *Name, Logo and Motto*. But before that, it must be said that brand management is not just a matter for large companies. Brand management concerns any company or institution in the consumer market. There are four types of brands! Product, service, certification and collective use brand. Positioning starts with the product, service or institution. The brand represents descriptive values that can be observed by the way the consumer reacts to certain offers in the market. As such, brand planning starts with three extremely significant elements. These elements are related and have relationships with each other. There are several examples that we can mention, but it is worth saying at this point that the brand's success starts exactly with the planning and development of these three elements. Let's see!

Figure 1

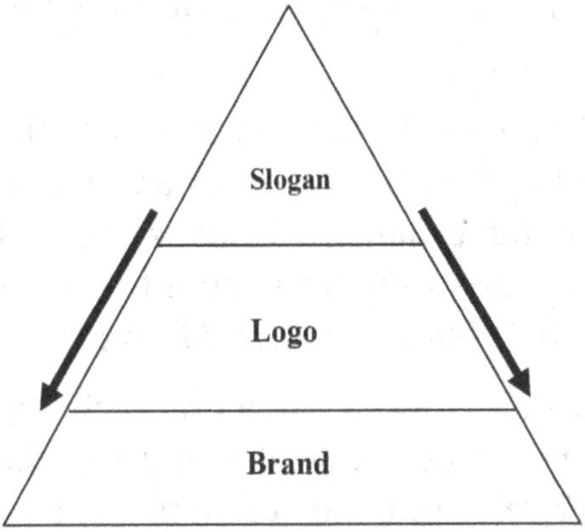

Data source: Global Consulting

According to the figure, the brand is at the base of the pyramid. Next comes the logo and then the slogan. It is essential to say that Branding is not just about creating the brand, but also about the management, and governance of the brand in the market. I've always said that Branding is a mental, rational, emotional process and not exactly a process of creation, design and communication. Thus, there are some criteria that are fundamental in creating a brand.

According to Kotler and Keller (2006), we basically have six criteria that can be used in creating a brand.

Memorable, meaningful, desirable, transferable, adaptable and protected. The first three can be characterized as a management process in terms of brand positioning and recognition. The last three are characterized according to market opportunities and limitations. Let's see!

Memorable - As the name says, it is the one easily remembered. Ex: *LG, HP, Apple, Sony, BMW, IBM etc.*

Significant - To what extent can the product or service be credible and indicative for the corresponding category? Does it suggest anything about branding or consumer behavior? Ex: *Sempre Livre absorbent, Gillette prestobarb, Zero-Cal sweetener, Colgate toothpaste, etc.*

Desirable - To what extent can we say the brand is attractive or desirable? Ex: *Johnnie Walker, Lamborghini, Ferrari, Marlboro etc.*

Transferable - To what extent does the brand collaborate with positioning in other countries and market segments? When using a transferable name it is advisable that these names only have a specific meaning in the country of origin. Ex: *Havaianas Sandals, Bombril, Ipanema, Leite Moça etc.*

Adaptable - How far can a brand change? There are brands that have gone through several changes in their look and despite being 60 or 70 years old, they seem to be at most 40 years old. Ex: *Everlast, Citibank, Coca-Cola, Salton, Ford etc.*

Protected - To what extent can a brand be protected? Can it be protected from competition? Can it be copied? Ex: *Microsoft, Google, Xiaomi etc.*

We cannot forget that the brand is an indicator of trust and credibility. For that reason, these brand elements are critical, particularly in the global marketplace. After choosing the name, the next step is to create a logo. Therefore, the logo becomes the graphic representation of the brand. For this, a broader vision is needed. Company values and characteristics must be reflected in the brand logo.

Some logos are actually a mix of nominative and figurative. In this case, the correct designation is logo. Both complete and intensify as they become known or recognized by consumers. Mixed use is usually not advisable, as the logo loses its main characteristic, that is, associating the product or service with the brand.

After the logo is the turn of the motto or slogan. The motto also plays an extremely significant role on the brand, and its main objective is to create differences in the consumer market. Even though it cannot represent everything the brand wants, the motto contributes a lot to the brand's positioning and image. If a motto cannot connect directly to the brand, then there is no point in creating a motto.

Choosing the motto is just as important as choosing the brand!

If the goal of the motto is to create differences, then that is the goal of the brand. The motto usually represents the central idea of the positioning and, therefore, the expectations of the company or institution regarding the product or service. Thus, the motto is an essential part of the brand structure and needs to be used whenever necessary. However, the motto must be part of the consumer's daily life, that is, it must be in the local context and never in the global context. Let's see!

Coca-Cola in the global context **(Taste the Feeling)**. In Brazil **(Sinta o sabor).**

McDonald's in the global context **(I'm lovin'it).** In Brazil **(Amo muito tudo isso).**

L'Oréal Paris in the global context **(Parce que vous le valez bien).** In Brazil **(Por que você vale muito).**

Brand Strategic Planning

Branding is an increasingly important tool in the economic scenario, after all, consumers do not buy products, but brands. We live in an economy of products, services and brands. However, which product or service effectively satisfies the consumer's needs, desires and expectations? This is a very important question. However, it is up to the market to respond impartially. The brand is made up of three factors that complete and complement each other. **Market, Segmentation and Positioning.** It is noteworthy that brand positioning has been neglected for years because of predatory communication. It is often necessary to ask the consumer, what is their expectation in relation to the product or service. Communication usually proposes an industry-formatted product. Often different from the needs, desires and expectations of the consumer market.

The mental model practiced in the market sustains that advertising is the best tool to position a brand in the market. However, advertising and brand positioning are different tools. Communication is important, but it does not mean meeting needs, desires and expectations. Brand management is a marketing function and not necessarily a communication function. Thus, it is not possible to correctly position a brand without effectively satisfying the consumer's needs, desires and expectations. Exchange processes and relations take place based on this concept and not just advertising actions. Let's see!

Figure 1.1

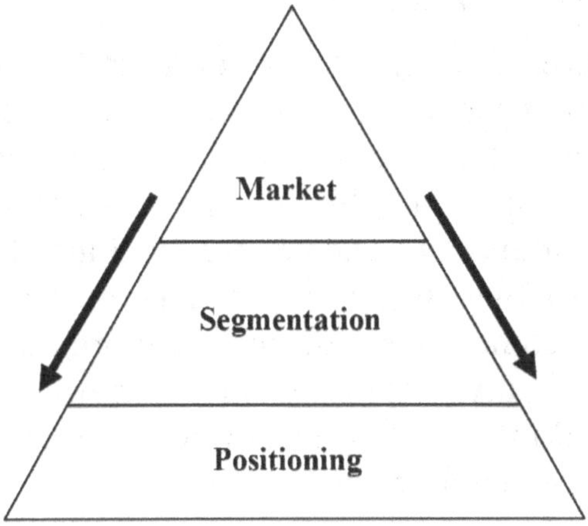

Data source: Global Consulting

According to the figure, the positioning is at the base of the pyramid, because it represents the needs and desires of the market. Thus, considering brand management in terms of advertising seems too shallow and tends to minimize brand longevity. In the goods industry, the brand represents the production and transformation processes of the product. Therefore, the brand's objective is to reduce complexity, due to the brand's ability to transmit relevant information to the consumer market. For example, we don't understand anything about the technology, engineering, architecture of the brands *BMW, Ferrari, Porsche, Lamborghini etc.* However, we blindly trust these brands. Hence the reason for the blind spot concept in the manufacturing industry.

Product Line Extension

From now on, we are going to talk about an extremely important subject in the global market. Line extension. But first, we need to establish the brand's strategic planning concept. It is the formal knowledge of all possible actions of a brand, whose objective is to manage the image and positioning of the product or service in the consumer market.

The diversification strategy and market expansion are two very important factors. In this way, line extension becomes a fundamental tool, and at the same time becomes an indicator of the brand's trust and credibility. The greater the recognition and awareness of the brand, the greater the line's chances of success. For basic products and services or commodities, the business name of the company is extremely important. Commodities are understood as any product or service that cannot be physically differentiated in the consumer's mind. Ex: *Ham, Meat, Chicken, Mayonnaise, Ketchup etc.*

Assuming a company decides to brand its products and services it must then choose which brand names to use. However, it is important to say that the strength of the brand is the fact that consumers do not consider all brands to be the same. A classic example is the white line (microwaves, stoves, washers, refrigerators, etc.). In the so-called white line, there are no significant product differences. This means that the difference is basically in the brand. Ex: *Consul, Brastemp, Electrolux, LG etc.* For this reason, brand management in the white goods is extremely important. In general, the white line needs to go beyond the brand, that is, have characteristics such as quality, design, durability, practicality and technology. Consumer mental status is another must-have tool in the white goods.

Brand Name Strategies

According to Kotler and Keller (2006), there are four naming strategies that are used in the market. Individual names, family names, separate family names for all products and company names or brand matching different products and services. Let's see!

Individual names - This strategy is widely used, as the company does not link its image to the product. If the product fails or is of inferior quality, the company's name and image are not harmed. Procter & Gamble is a company that uses this strategy successfully. Ex: *Gillette, Oral-B, Ariel, Pantene, Downy, Always, Pampers etc.*

Family names - This strategy is also used a lot, as a family name has its advantages. The cost of planning and development is low, as there is no need to research names or spend on advertising to make the brand more comprehensive. Nestlé is a company that uses this strategy successfully. Ex: ***Nescafé, Nescau, Neston, Nesfit, Nesquik, Nespresso*** *etc.* The initials of the products always refer to the company's commercial name (Nestlé).

Separate family names - This strategy is adopted when the company develops different products, in which case it is not advisable to use a comprehensive family name. McDonalds is a company that uses this strategy successfully. Ex: *McChicken, McLanche Feliz (Brazil), McFlurry KitKat etc.*

Company brand combining with different products and services - This strategy is widely used in the market. The company's brand reflects trust and credibility and the name identifies the product. Peugeot is a company that uses this strategy successfully. However, instead of using names, it uses numbers. Ex: *Peugeot 208, 308, 2008, 3008 etc.*

Portfolio Analysis

With line extension, another extremely important issue comes up. Portfolio analysis. The portfolio is the set of all brands and lines that a company offers to buyers in the same category. When developing a portfolio, it is essential to analyze the scope of the market. If profits can be increased by increasing the number of brands, it means that the portfolio has not yet reached the company's market potential. On the other hand, if profits can be increased by reducing the number of brands, it means that the portfolio is too big.

The basic principle of the portfolio is to maintain a balance between market coverage and brand overlap. For this reason, there are brands that can be considered strategic, as they represent a challenge and, at the same time, a market opportunity. These brands are usually recognized by consumers due to their price, prestige, profitability and competitiveness. There are four branding strategies that are commonly used in the market. Fighting Brands, Profitable Brands, Cheapest Entry Brands and Prestige Brands. Let's see!

Figure 1.2

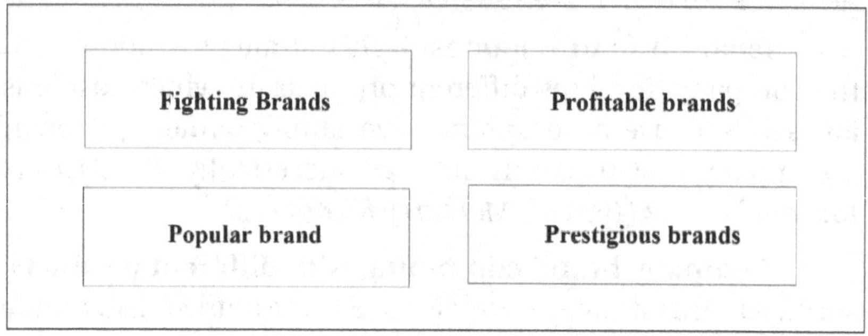

Data source: Global Consulting

Fighting brands - As the name says, it is positioned in relation to competitors, so that the leading brand maintains the desired positioning. When creating a fighting brand, it is necessary to develop a critical sense regarding the market itself. The combatant brand must not be related to other brands in the portfolio. However, if it is, it should not reflect inferiority in the market.

Profitable brands - It is the one that manages to maintain its profitability without any marketing support. This means that the brand effectively meets the needs, desires and expectations of the consumer market. Ex: *Nestlé, Apple, LG, Samsung, Electrolux, Google, General Eletric etc.*

Popular brand - Also known as "cheaper entry brand", it aims to attract the target market. The popular brand is a kind of fundamental gimmick in any company.

Prestigious brands - As the name says, it is the relatively most expensive brand in the portfolio. The objective is to add prestige and credibility to the production and transformation processes of the company's product, brand or trade name. Ex: *Jaguar, Lamborghini, Porsche, BMW, Ferrari etc.*

The next step is to know the brand's recognition rate in the market. This is an extremely important step, as there is no strong brand without an index or value indicator. *Top of mind* market research is the tool used to measure this index. However, research should not only focus on brand recall, but also on consumer motivations and experiences. It is worth saying that the relationship with the brand is also an extremely important tool. Features such as durability, technology, design, practicality and comfort are important mental statuses. Brands considered prestigious should reflect the consumer's mental status and connect the structures in memory, in the face of the brand's transformation processes.

Brand Equity

Research can often reveal important data, which shows that brand management is an important tool in the consumer's daily life as well. There are several research institutes. However, the help of a professional or company specialized in brand management is necessary. Later, we'll look at why market research is an important tool. Brand Equity reflects the very concept of marketing, that is, meeting needs, desires and expectations. Consumer loyalty is directly related to this concept. The future value of the brand comprises the nature, concepts and ways of understanding the consumer's desire for the company's commercial name. The capital market represents significant tangible values, which need to be dimensioned and represented by numbers, graphs and reports that reveal the importance and tradition of the brand in the market. Hence the reason for the credibility of the financial market. Financial institutions and brokerages need market information such as corporate governance, relationships and, of course, the value that the brand represents in the global market. Let's see!

Figure 1.3

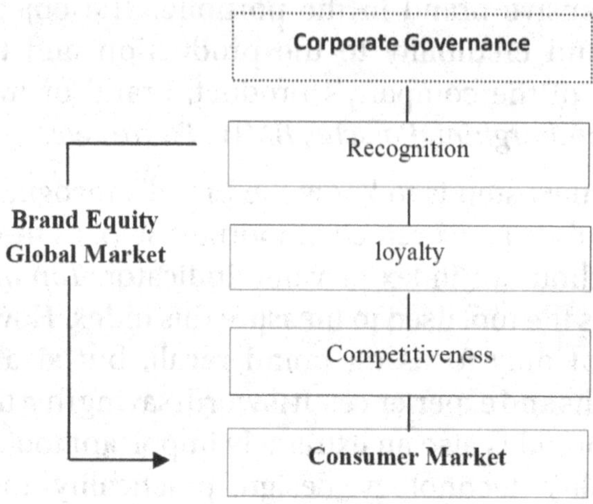

Data source: Global Consulting

The figure above represents opportunities and commitments of a company or financial institution. However, it is necessary to manage these values, as brand management is, above all, a mental, rational and emotional process. It is noteworthy that these values are related to each other, however, they concern both the tangible assets and the intangible assets of the brand. It must be remembered that quality is the backbone of brand value, and concerns the consumer's perception of the product or service. Recognition means satisfying the consumer's needs, desires and expectations. Loyalty means brand competitiveness and profitability. Mental statuses represent the consumer's feeling about the product, service or brand. The higher the status, the higher the level of brand recognition in the consumer market.

Annually, we have the disclosure of the most valuable brands in the world. It is important to pay attention to the dissemination of this information by the research institutes. The marketing analyst must pay attention to the changes in positioning and image, especially considering the strength of the brand on the digital platform.

Co-branding

The next step is a well-known strategy in the global market. Co-branding means a consortium between two brands in which neither of them could compete separately. This strategy brings us to the combination of strengths and weaknesses of the brand. To compensate for weaknesses, Co-branding is a very interesting strategy, as its objective is to make the brand recognition process more effective. However, this strategy concerns different market segments, that is, the union of two brands in different segments. Recognition is therefore in the segment where the brand needs a strong perception or concept in the market. Ex: *Visa / Mastercard, etc.*

Product Life Cycle Analysis

Now we'll look at another extremely important step in brand positioning. In any company, analyzing the product life cycle is fundamental. It is necessary to analyze the life cycle considering not only the product's useful life, but factors that exert influence during the cycle. These factors are related to lifestyle, fashion, fad or trend. Due to the constant process of innovation, it is also necessary to analyze the market life cycle, as market demand is also influenced by these factors. Let's see!

Figure 1.4

Product Life Cycle

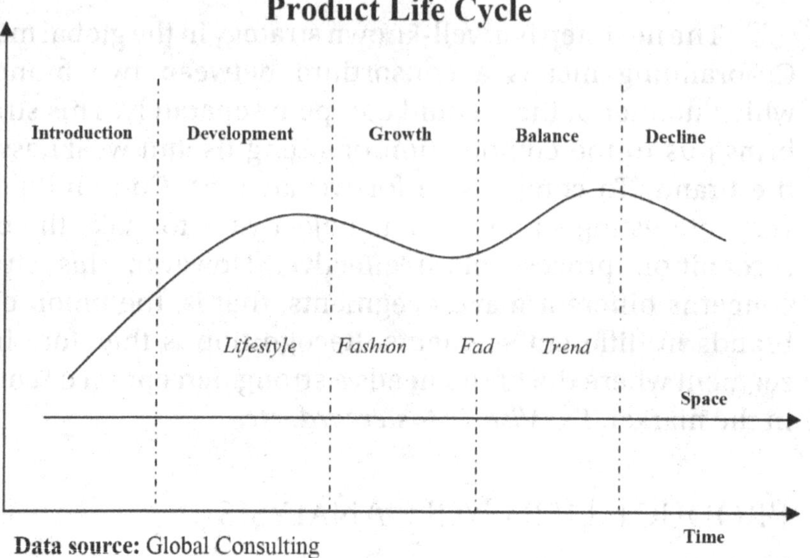

Data source: Global Consulting

The figure above is crucial for understanding the differences in the market in general. Every product or service goes through the phase of introduction, development, growth, balance and, consequently, decline. Brand positioning starts right at the intro phase. If there is a flaw in the positioning, obviously, the target market will be confused. But if the company's positioning was successful it will be easy to position the product or service. Thus, positioning is the action of fixing the product or service in the target market.

After the introduction of the brand comes the development phase. It is necessary to consider an average time of five to ten years between one phase and another, depending on the company's financial structure. In the development phase, the brand begins to gain strength and recognition in the target market. In the growth phase, the brand begins to conquer a larger portion of the market, that is, the brand begins to occupy a differentiated place in the consumer's mind. In the equilibrium phase, we can say that the brand is already well known and, for this reason, there is no need for so much communication, advertising or publicity, except in cases of market leadership. Remembering that, according to the segment, we have several different forms of communication and positioning.

On the other hand, the company cannot be held hostage to communication. The psychological effect that advertising causes often, causes some distrust and imbalance in the market. That's because advertising doesn't satisfy the needs, desires and expectations of the consumer. The best advertising is the quality and governance of the brand in the market.

Even in the growth or expansion phase of the market, it is essential to make clear the objective of the brand's positioning. The result of positioning must be the creation of value (status), that is, a clear reason why the consumer should buy the product or service. In the equilibrium phase, the company needs to avoid commoditizing the product or brand. To avoid commoditization, it is necessary to follow the concept of positioning, that is, to create significant differences. It is necessary to create an atmosphere a different! It is extremely important to inform consumers why the brand is different, especially in the balancing phase. Here are four tools a company can use to differentiate a brand. Let's see!

Product Dimension - Brands can be differentiated based on a number of factors. Among which we can highlight the durability, practicality, design and technology.

Dimension of service - Brands can be differentiated based on services. Providing quality service is increasingly important in the target market. The company needs to offer a service compatible with the consumer's expectations.

Distribution Channel Dimension - Brands can be differentiated based on the distribution channel. Often, what we really need is to establish an efficient sales channel. A few years ago, pet food was cheap, poorly nutritious and sold exclusively in supermarkets. Today, we can find it in various places, with different flavors and nutritional values and in specialty stores (Pet Shops).

Brand dimension - Brands can be differentiated according to image dimension and positioning. How a company seeks to position the brand is extremely important. The company needs to establish the brand's personality and communicate that personality in a differentiated way. For the brand's identity or name to be successful, it must be conveyed to the public through all types of communication, especially on the digital platform. If the *Red Bull* brand means relaxation of the mind, this message must be expressed in all the brand's media.

Additionally, it is essential to consider some factors outside the life cycle. These factors influence the product life cycle and, at the same time, the consumer market. Thus, we need to consider the timeline or cycle as a parameter in the target market. As technology advances, a new product/market cycle begins. The trend is to have an increasingly shorter cycle because of the amount of products and services on the market. It is also important to say that brand dynamics dictate rules in the consumer market. Therefore, the brand occupies a denser space in human thought.

It is essential to know exactly the influence of these factors on the product or service life cycle, considering the fad as a common factor without much expression in the market's life cycle. On the other hand, we need to consider *technology* and *innovation* as the market *thermometer*. The objective is to measure the level of demand evolution. It is noteworthy that the market is going through several changes, and it is perfectly possible to follow these changes with the analysis of the product's life cycle. However, by analyzing the product lifecycle we can better understand the market lifecycle. For this reason, it is essential to make the product or service tangible in the consumer's mind. Making tangible necessarily means offering a quality product or service. On the other hand, it is also necessary to consider the time and space for renewal of each cycle, product or service in the consumer market.

ANALYSIS OF GROWTH OPPORTUNITIES IN THE MARKET

We come to another important point in the brand's strategic planning. According to Kotler and Keller (2006), there are four strategies used to define growth opportunities, also called intensive growth. These actions combined with the practice of Branding give rise to a new marketing concept, now with an emphasis on brand positioning. Let's see!

Figure 1.5

Intensive Brand Growth

Current product + Current market	*Market Penetration*
Current market + New product	*Product Development*
Current product + New market	*Market Development*
New Product + New Market	*Diversification*

Data source: Global Consulting

Based on the figure, we can see that each strategy can be used in the market, however, with a focus on brand positioning. All aspects of this thought are based on the concept of marketing. We will analyze each strategy and how they can assist the company in planning and developing new products, services and brands. Let's see!

Figure 1.6

Market Penetration

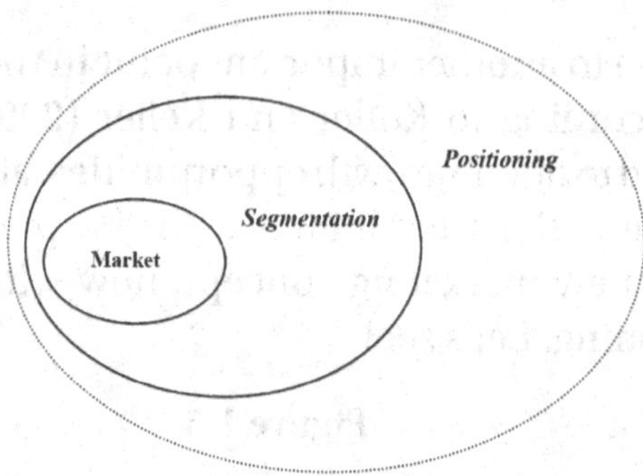

Data source: Global Consulting

Looking at the figure, we have three essential elements in each specific business or project. The first concerns target market penetration. However, there are three questions we must ask before any product or service: *What exactly does the market want? Because wants? And how do you want it?* These questions are extremely significant and bring us back to the very concept of marketing. However, this process is also related to the market lifecycle, because of the brand's level of competition. Let's see!

Figure 1.7

Market Lifecycle

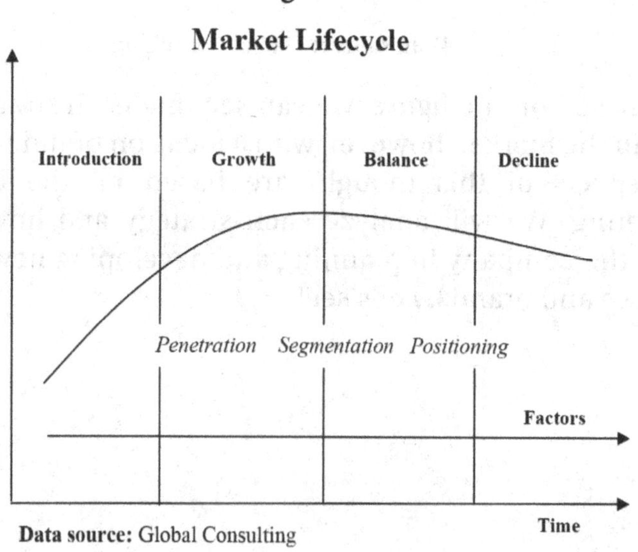

Data source: Global Consulting

Based on the figure, the market goes through the stages of introduction, growth, maturity and decline. Each stage is influenced by the level of demand. In this way, the market is directly influenced by the consumer's purchasing decisions. The first step is to create a customer database with accurate information about behavior, purchase decision and lifestyle. In this way, the company can keep up with the changes that are constantly taking place in the target market. However, it is also necessary to consider the factors that influence the market life cycle. Factors such as *Fashion, Fad, Lifestyle and Trend* are extremely important facts, especially in the introduction and market growth phase.

The second step concerns market segmentation, that is, who are our consumers. It is essential to draw a socioeconomic profile, with information regarding the target market. We can draw a socioeconomic profile according to some demographic variables such as age, sex, income, education and stage of life. The stage of life is by far an extremely important variable in the target market. These variables are very significant and help us understand why brand management is an increasingly important tool in modern marketing.

The third step concerns exactly the positioning of the brand in the target market. It all starts with the product or service, and from that moment on, the company starts to project its image in the consumer's mind. In this sense, brand management becomes a mental and emotional process. For this reason, the brand is directly related to symbols, terms, signs, among other factors. The second strategy, that is, product development, aims to choose between the dimensions of the product, which dimension meets the needs and desires of the consumer market. This combination is extremely important and is directly related to the added value of the product or service. It is noteworthy that technology is an increasingly important dimension in the market, however, there are other dimensions that also exert a strong influence on purchasing decisions and consumer behavior. Let's see!

Figure 1.8

Product or Service Dimension

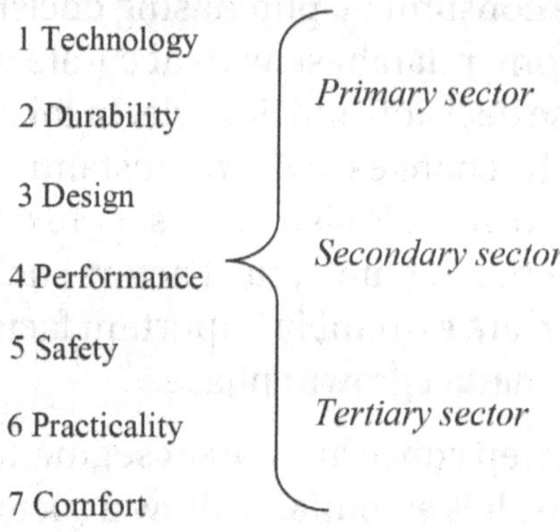

Data Source: Global Consulting

Looking at the figure, we realize how important the product dimensions are and how much they exert a direct influence on the brand's positioning. It's like a puzzle in which we need to perfectly match the dimensions of each product. This combination determines the degree of efficiency of the product or brand (competitive advantage). However, this same combination can also be applied to the service sector. However, not all dimensions of the product are compatible with offering services in the consumer market. However, it is important to say that the service is present in each specific sector of the economy. The service is the highlight in the primary, secondary and tertiary sectors. For this reason, the service is considered the driver of the world economy. Without service, there are no inputs, finished product and, above all, improvement in quality of life and self-esteem. However, we can say that intuition is an important factor in the consumer market. The greater the consumer's intuition or interaction with the product, the greater the chances of the corporate brand's success in the market.

The third strategy, that is, market development, aims to meet the needs of a specific group of consumers or market niche. However, the brand will be desired by satisfying the entire niche. This means that competition is a factor that must be considered in the niche market. Often, the company seeks to meet a certain market niche, and ends up discovering that it is actually serving the market itself.

Figure 1.9

Market Development Strategy

Data source: Global Consulting

According to the figure, we clearly perceive the importance of the niche to the target market. It is critical to consider the consumer's lifestyle before considering the niche market. For example, the elderly is a group with specific needs, so it is a market niche and, eventually, a specific market segment. Let's see!

Figura 1.10

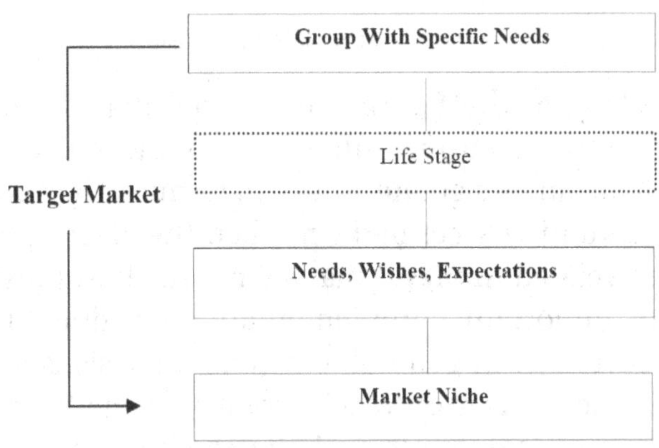

Data source: Global Consulting

Based on the figure, we realize that before developing the market or niche, it is necessary to follow a line of thought, as the market is composed of a set of buyers and sellers. In this sense, it is essential to consider who the buyers are, as the consumer's stage of life becomes an extremely significant variable. Depending on the consumer's life stage, needs and priorities are extremely different.

The fourth strategy, that is, diversification aims to increase market share through diversification or line extension. The diversification strategy is very important, however, the brand needs to create significant differences from the target market. Let's see!

Figure 1.11

Diversification Strategy

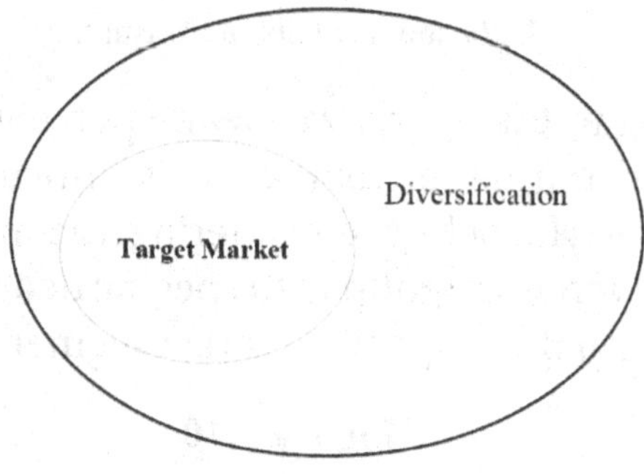

Data source: Global Consulting

Looking at the figure, we can see that the diversification strategy exerts a strong influence on the consumer. For this reason, it occupies a greater space in terms of the competitiveness of products and services in the market. The diversification strategy is directly related to brand management. Thus, portfolio analysis is a very important complementary tool, due to the level of market coverage. In general, portfolio analysis is very helpful in the diversification or outreach strategy of the brand. Hence the importance of maintaining a balance between market coverage and overlapping brands in the portfolio. Ex: *Procter & Gamble, Nestlé, Unilever, Johnson & Johnson etc.*

Finally, we have two more strategies that also represent growth opportunities. Integrated growth and Growth through diversification. Integrated growth is an increasingly important tool in the global market. Also known as the vertical market, integrated growth is responsible for most acquisitions and mergers in Brazil and worldwide. The brand's share or value in the financial market is related to integrated growth. On the other hand, the growing digital environment can monopolize the consumer market, as the digital environment has no borders. A classic example is the Chinese brand Alibaba! The "AliExpress" digital platform is a strong competitor in the global market. The *Amazon* platform is also another strong competitor in the global market.

Integrated growth is related to acquisition or merger processes. This means that the governance or management of the brand is fundamental both in the acquisition and in the merger, as it involves several factors related to the consumer market itself. Consumer behavior is a factor that must be considered, especially in mergers. Therefore, the company must favor the brand with the highest recognition rate in the market. The acquisition or merger has different personalities! The merger personality is different from the acquisition personality. Mental status is different regarding consumer behavior and purchasing decisions, especially in mergers. It is worth remembering that the digital platform is drastically changing the way the market is adapting to new vertical integration trends.

Growth by sectorial diversification or convergence is another tool that is also widely used. Brand penetration in other market segments is quite common. However, convergence is indicated when the structures, status and personality of the brand are compatible with the new market segment. Otherwise, brand convergence is not indicated. Often, the problem is not necessarily with the product, but with the brand. Ex: *Head & Shoulders, Listerine, Hershey's etc.* It must be remembered that descriptive names can make it difficult for sectorial convergence or brand convergence. On the other hand, it contributes a lot to the diversification strategy. Ex: *Microsoft, Boeing, Caterpillar, Pedigree, Havaianas, Movement, American Express, Mastercard, FedEx, General Electric, Starlink, Airbus, Motorola etc.*

It must be made clear that the diversification strategy is one thing and line extension is another. Line extension as the name says, is a line developed from a specific product. The diversification strategy is different, that is, it is a variety of products in different segments or business units. Let's see!

Figure 1.12

Growth by Diversification

Data source: Global Consulting

Looking closely at the figure, we realize how important growth through diversification is. We could never imagine, for example, that brands like *General Electric, Caterpillar, Yamaha, etc.* They could effectively be in other market segments. This therefore reflects market opportunities, competitiveness, and increasing competition in the global market. In this sense, the ideal is that the brand does not have any specific meaning in other languages. It is important to remember that the more complex the choice of a brand name, the greater the difficulty in positioning it. However, it is also necessary to remember that there are other means of growth or expansion of the brand. There are two forms of growth that are quite common in the global market. *Franchise* and *Licensing*! However, brand management follows the same principle, that it is necessary to create differences, especially with regard to the offer of services in the consumer market.

Finally, there are some names, last names of people, extremely important personalities in the global market. We have as an example the Italian football player, Leonardo Spinazzola. The **Spinazzola** surname is extremely suggestive as it can easily convert the brand in the consumer's mind. Ex: Instant *noodles, soy oil, gourmet sauce, butter, margarine, biscuits, french fries, jam, pate, cereals...* In short, a gigantic portfolio of food products!

Spinazzola is a fantastic name! Always up to date, modern and contemporary!

Another very suggestive surname is also from the Danish football player, Martin Braithwaite. The **Braithwaite** surname is extremely suggestive in the alcoholic and non-alcoholic beverages segment. Ex: *Whiskey, Vodka, Beer, Sports Drinks, Supplements, Energy Drink, Wine, Champagne, Mineral Water...* An excellent product portfolio!

Braithwaite is a successful name! A name that goes beyond the brand's expectations.

However, we can say that the football player's surname Andrés Iniesta, is also an excellent option. The **Iniesta** surname is very suggestive, especially in the automotive industry. Ex: *Ford Iniesta, Fiat Iniesta, Porsche Iniesta...* Iniesta is an extremely innovative name in the category and, at the same time, with a high potential for convergence in the consumer's mind.

MARKETING COMMUNICATION

Communication is the means by which companies seek to inform and guide consumers, directly or indirectly, about products, services and brands. Marketing communication represents the brand's aspirations, therefore, marketing communication collaborates with the image and positioning of the product or service in the target market. Even though advertising is the central element of communication, it is usually not the only or most important factor when it comes to brand management.

The communication mix consists of six different forms of use in the market. Let's see!

Advertising - Any form of non-personal presentation and promotion of ideas, products, services and brands.

Sales Promotion - A variety of short-term incentives to estimate the behavior of a product or service.

Events - Company-sponsored activities and programs to create interactions related to products, services and brands.

Public relations and press relations - Variety of programs aimed at promoting or protecting the image of a company, product or service.

Direct marketing - use of communication or digital platform for direct communication with the consumer or customer.

Personal sales - Personal interaction (door to door) with the consumer or customer. The objective is to present products and services outside the traditional market environment.

How brand associations reach the market does not matter. However, marketing activities must be integrated in order to convey an image consistent with the brand's positioning. To what extent, for example, can an advertisement contribute to brand equity awareness?

From a brand point of view, marketers must evaluate all possible communication actions that really interest, or might interest the target audience. Communication visibility suggests that activities can be especially valuable in optimizing brand awareness. However, improving recall can suggest a more intense and well-structured process. In this way, stronger ties to the brand or category of products and services can improve awareness of the brand's goals. All possible marketing communication options must be analyzed, with the aim of creating brand awareness and image in the consumer's mind.

COMMUNICATION PROCESS

There are two models of marketing communication. Macro model and Micro model.

The template macro contains some elements. Two of them represent the parties involved in the commercialization, that is, the sender and the receiver. Two others represent the main functions of communication, such as encoding and decoding. The last element of the system is noise (random messages that can interfere with communication). The model emphasizes the main factors of communication. The sender needs to know what audience he wants to reach and what reactions he wants to generate. It must also encode the message for the target audience to decode it.

The micro communication model focuses on specific consumer responses. The learn-feel-act sequence is appropriate when the audience is heavily involved with a product category that seems too broad and heterogeneous. The act-feel-learn sequence is important when the audience is highly involved with the product but perceives little or no differentiation between relatively low-priced products in the consumer market.

We will show a communication model and its effects on the consumer market. Let's use, as an example, a health plan operator.

Blue Health Operator (fictional)!

Awareness - In this case, the task of the communicator is to develop awareness, taking into account mainly the quality of the service.

Ex: *Blue Health, reference in service in the United States!*

Knowledge - The target market is aware of the brand, but doesn't know anything about it. It is then necessary to guide and inform the market about the brand's products and services. It is essential to emphasize the services that the operator (Blue Health) offers, and what the brand's competitive differential is.

Friendliness - Friendliness for the brand is an important competitive advantage. Therefore, it is advisable for the brand to be descriptive or meaningful, depending on the market segment.

Preference - The choice of brand is a very important decision. Thus, the focus must always be on brand positioning. Positioning, in this specific case, means that the brand is focused on offering high-performance service and customer service. Obviously, the preference is for the service and, eventually, for the technology or market platform used. Thus, communication should focus on the service model and not necessarily on tangible brand values.

DEVELOPMENT OF MARKETING COMMUNICATION

Let's now show you some important steps for a good marketing communication plan. Let's see!

Identification of the target audience:

Identifying the target audience is actually segmenting the communication. Which target audience reached? Which target audience is not reached? Communication cannot overlook the possibility of segmenting the brand, taking into account different audiences. The billboard, for example, needs to reach different audiences. Therefore, instead of emphasizing just the product or service, marketing communication needs to focus on different audiences or market segments, using the same communication model.

Preparation of communication:

The communication process requires solving three problems: What exactly to say (message strategy), how to say it (creative strategy), and who to say it (message source).

Message strategy

In this case, the creative side of marketing can help a lot. A creative advertisement can contribute a lot to the image and positioning of the brand.

Ex: Absorbent Always Free! (Conveys the idea of freedom).

Ex: Silk Shampoo! (Conveys the idea of softness).

Ex: Zero-Cal Sweetener! (Conveys the idea of fewer calories).

Ex: Google Android! (Conveys the idea of technology).

Ex: Disney! (Conveys the idea of entertainment).

Thus, the message source must be in harmony with the image and with the brand's positioning in the target market.

Creative strategy

The effectiveness of communication often depends on how the message is expressed. Creative strategy defines how marketers translate their messages into creative messages. Let's see!

Informational appeals

The appeal is a tool that can help you define your marketing communication plan.

Ex: Doril (Took Doril, the pain disappeared).

Ex: SBP (Terrible against insects, against insects!).

Ex: Bombril (1001 utilities).

In this way, the informational appeal can show a direction, driving the marketing communication, optimizing time and financial resources in advertising and publicity.

Message source

Message font is an extremely important tool. Many brands prefer to use a font already known on the market. Thus, source credibility is often the backbone of marketing communication. On the other hand, it is necessary to take into account a number of factors such as segmentation, brand identity, positioning, product lifecycle, service offering and market lifecycle.

The surprise factor is also an essential tool for those on the other side, that is, the recipient of the message. Try to imagine famous artists in their 70s doing commercials for sports cars, condoms, contraceptives, etc.

It is often necessary to overcome the barrier of brand positioning!

SELECTION OF COMMUNICATION CHANNELS

Today there are several means and channels of communication. Market penetration is not always easy, as the level of competition in the market is very high. At this point, it is necessary to select a good communication channel, taking into account the size of the target audience. It is important to remember that the quality of the product or service is still the best advertisement. Before deciding to invest resources in an advertising campaign, it is necessary to make sure that the product or service has quality. Otherwise, it's no use investing in communication and marketing.

Remember, the worst thing in life is false advertising!

It is no use trying to deceive the consumer, this rule does not apply to the market. The future value of the brand necessarily depends on the awareness and transparency of communication.

Ex: *Colgate Total 12 toothpaste! The brand promises 12 benefits in a single product! It's possible?*

Is the brand elasticity in the communication?

Thus, the success of any brand begins in the production and transformation processes of the product or service. No matter the means of communication, it is essential to consider the image and brand positioning in the consumer's mind and, eventually, in the media. Does the product have quality? Does the service have quality? What really matters is the quality, not just the way the information is conveyed to the target audience.

Important Tip:

The service industry has definitely incorporated the entertainment industry. We can say with certainty that tourism is an entertainment industry and, eventually, an economic activity. Entertainment brands such as: *Disney, Google, Netflix...* It shows very clearly and objectively, because entertainment is today a huge potential market in relation to the transformation industry. In other words, this means that entertainment brands tend to dominate the service sector mainly due to the significant increase in demand and brand repositioning. The entertainment market will completely dominate the services sector due to the advancement of technology, digital platform and customer service model.

CHAPTER 2

STRATEGIC MARKETING PLANNING

Planning is a way to organize ideas in relation to a certain topic, and establish objectives and goals with the purpose of achieving an expected result. We can say that it is also a way to predict the future, taking into account environmental factors such as strengths and weaknesses, or even opportunities and threats of the brand. Obviously, we are talking about strategic planning. Planning can be represented as follows:

Figure 2.1

Data source: Global Consulting

Analyzing the figure, we come to the conclusion that planning is a fundamental tool in the company's daily activities. Operational planning must be among the company's premises. The focus on the human element is essential, as the human being is endowed with feelings and emotions, unlike technology. We will now look at the marketing plan, which in practice also includes the concept of strategic planning.

MARKETING AND CONCEPTS

Are we going to fix some concepts about marketing?

What is marketing?

The purpose of marketing is to know the customer or target market. There are several current concepts for the word marketing, however, Kotler's concept seems more appropriate to the theme, as in addition to needs and desires, we can also add expectations, especially taking into account the brand's image and positioning in the market. Thus, marketing is a human activity aimed at satisfying needs, desires and expectations, in the face of exchange processes (Kotler, 1980).

Trading and Marketing

There are four alternatives for getting a product. A person can produce his own food by hunting, fishing or gathering fruit. He can use physical strength to get what he needs. You can ask for charity, like the homeless, or you can use something as a bargaining chip. We can say that exchange is the central concept of marketing. Exchange is the most common alternative in the market and involves two parts that we can call supply and demand. For the exchange to take place, at least four considerations are necessary. First, that there are at least two parts. Second, that the parties have something of value to each other. Third, that the parties have the power to communicate and deliver. Fourth, that the parties believe it is appropriate to participate in the negotiation.

WHO IS MARKETING INTENDED FOR

Marketing can be aimed at products, services, people, places and organizations. However, it is necessary to know the target market or demand well. There are seven types of demand on the market. Let's see!

Negative Demand - It is when there is no interest in the product or service.

Non-existent demand - This is when the product or service is not yet known, or when consumers are not interested in it.

Latent demand - This is a desirable demand, however, there is still no product or service on the market to meet this demand.

Declining demand - This is when consumers gradually stop buying the product or service.

Irregular demand - It is the demand that can vary according to the needs, desires and expectations of the market.

Full demand - It is the demand that does not vary in relation to the supply, that is, the supply is equal to the demand.

Excessive demand - It is the demand that goes beyond the supply or the capacity to supply the target market.

The market is a set of consumers and companies! The main customer markets are consumer, organizational, global and non-profit market. The digital platform has been changing the way the market relates to the consumer. This change is basically technological and digital. The digital platform is the gateway to new services and increased competition. We are not just talking about technology! We are talking about a corporate market that moves billions of dollars.

HOW MARKETING IS CHANGING

The only certainty we have is that today's market will not be tomorrow's due to the product's life cycle. This process is quite impactful, especially from the consumer's point of view. This basically means that the change in the product's life cycle causes constant changes in the consumer market. These are the main changes in the global market. Let's see!

Technological Change - As soon as new technologies become available, there will certainly be significant changes in the corporate market. It is necessary to consider technology as an important factor in the market lifecycle.

Globalization - Globalization and the international market are other factors that cause significant changes in the local market. Nowadays it is much easier to connect products and services through the digital platform. This means increased competition in virtually every sector of the economy. Globalization has caused a certain dissipation in the market, given uncontrollable factors such as the advancement of digital technology.

Customization - Customization, despite not being a trend, exerts a certain influence on the market. The possibility of customizing products and services is an important competitive advantage, especially considering some sectors such as information technology.

Sectoral convergence - Sectoral convergence or growth through diversification is another interesting factor that has caused significant changes in the global context. The brand can occupy significant space in the consumer's mind. Therefore, convergence is a fundamental marketing strategy in view of the advancement of technology and increased competition.

Disintermediation - The internet caused a certain euphoria in the market, and with it also disintermediation or deregulation. What used to be regular within the transformation industry and the service industry has become something basically cosmetic due mainly to the digital environment.

Acquisition and merger - The growing digital environment and the advancement of information technology, caused a massive growth in the number of acquisitions and mergers in the global market. The merger allows for greater competitiveness in the consumer market. On the other hand, the acquisition allows for greater brand participation in different market segments.

Economic sustainability - The planet's economy necessarily depends on new sources of clean and sustainable energy. The energy sector will be the most competitive on the planet. Energy and economic sustainability will be the main highlight and competitive differential in the government corporate market.

MARKETING ORIENTATION FOR THE MARKET

Marketing has already been seen as an area of sales, communication, distribution, etc. Now we need to guide marketing so that the market can have access to the brand's production and transformation processes. Today, the focus is not only on the product, price, communication and logistics, but mainly on the image and positioning of the brand. The brand is a kind of umbrella (sombrero), whose objective is to protect the production and transformation processes to which the brand undergoes. This protection is what we can call brand trust and credibility. We can cite, for example, the product lifecycle, the market lifecycle, growth opportunities, competitive analysis and brand communication.

This basically means that today the market is oriented towards the brand, whether it is a product, service, certification or collective use. The market is in tune with everything that reflects the perceptions of the consumer or customer. This is the principle of brand management, but it goes beyond the creation of names, symbols, colors and mottos. Therefore, this is the new orientation of modern marketing, a more contemporary vision, centered on the brand concept and not just on communication. Therefore, the concept of [1]blind spot in the manufacturing industry is extremely important, as it reveals a sense of belonging, trust and credibility. A concept that transcends the very existence of future value, intangibles, positioning, but which has a strong influence on purchasing decisions and consumer behavior.

---

1 The blind spot concept in the manufacturing industry is fundamental, as the consumer is unaware of the brand's transformation process. For this reason, the only source of trust and credibility is the brand's image and positioning in the market.

MARKETING PLAN

The process of creating, integrating and communicating value requires marketing expertise. To ensure that the plan is well structured it is essential that there is a strategic plan. The marketing plan requires action in three important areas. The first is to manage each business with a focus on the market's needs, desires and expectations. The second involves evaluating the strengths of each business within the company. The third is to develop a marketing strategy, that is, strategic, tactical and operational planning. To understand marketing management it is essential to understand strategic planning.

Each division establishes a plan for resource allocation within the business unit. Each business unit develops a marketing plan, which takes into account medium and long-term objectives. The strategic plan establishes the target audience based on an analysis of the best opportunities in the market. Tactical planning is responsible for outlining marketing tactics, including product features, service, pricing, communication, and sales channels.

CORPORATE STRATEGIC PLANNING

By establishing the mission, objectives, and goals, you can determine the framework within which divisions and business units can determine the strategic plan.

Definition of corporate mission:

To define a mission, the company must answer the following question: What is our business? Who is our customer? What do we have of value to the customer? The mission must be part of the company's daily life. A well-shared mission can better guide the goals of the company or institution. Typically, mission statements are based on two important points. First point! Focus on limited number of goals.

Ex: *We will manufacture the best products in the world and offer the best services and sales channels.*

This is a goal that the company may not be able to achieve, especially considering the scarcity of human resources. Second point! The mission should also emphasize the values and essence of the company's brand or trade name.

Ex: *Offer products and services aligned with the brand's image and positioning in the market.*

Business definition:

It is essential to define the business philosophy well. For this, it is important to know the reason, the existence of the brand in the consumer's mind. It is very common for entrepreneurs to lose focus and competitiveness in the market, precisely, for not defining the reason or motivation for the business.

What is the reason for the deal? Product or service?

Organization and organizational culture:

The organization of a company is based on its structure, policy and organizational culture. However, it is difficult to change the corporate culture, unlike the organizational structure or policy. But what does corporate culture mean? Just by entering a company or institution, we can already perceive the brand's business culture.

The mission and vision, setting objectives and goals, macro-environmental analysis or SWOT analysis, strategy formulation, implementation and control can help to better define the marketing plan or business strategy. Let's see!

Figure 2.2

Marketing plan

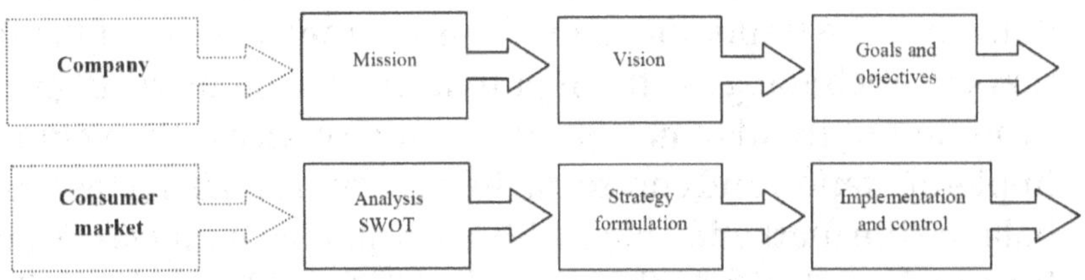

Data source: Global Consulting

Following the premises of the marketing plan, we came to the conclusion that it is divided into two aspects. The first is the company, where it is necessary to define the mission, vision, objectives and goals to be achieved. The second concerns the consumer market, where it is necessary to analyze the strengths and weaknesses of the brand, as well as the opportunities and threats, taking into account the uncontrollable forces, that is, the economic, political, social, cultural and sustainable environment. Then comes the definition of marketing strategies. This is the most difficult part, as it is necessary to take into account several factors inherent to the market itself. In other words, this means that it is essential to analyze the changes that are constantly taking place in the consumer market. Let's see!

Figure 2.3

Market lifecycle

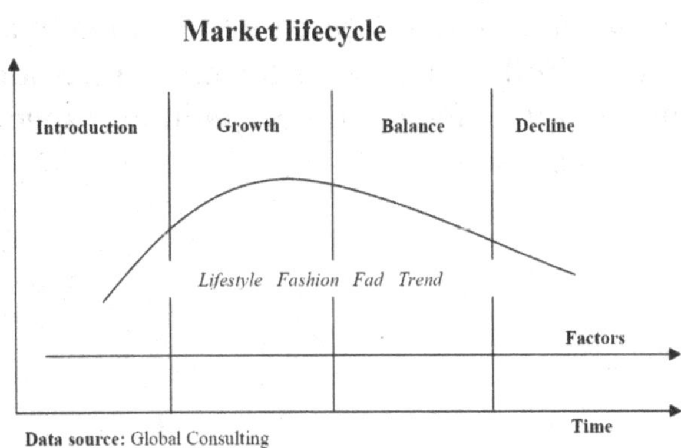

Data source: Global Consulting

Hese factors may explain why the market is so dispersed. Rivalry or agreement can be justified from the moment the fad, fashion, style or trend are part of the consumer's or customer's daily life. The trend, for example, is a strong feature of the digital market. Technology is the fuel that moves the market, given the evolution or trend of new products and services. Then comes the implementation and control of the marketing plan. It is essential to balance the marketing plan with the available financial resources. It must be asked whether the plan is feasible, both inside and outside the organization. It is necessary to have a more cautious view, especially taking into account the view from the outside, that is, the view of the market, the consumer or the customer.

COMPETITION ANALYSIS

Success is our biggest competitor!

"In a competitive and fragmented world, brand management is not the only factor capable of overcoming the competition. In this environment, cost-effectiveness becomes an extremely important tool, in terms of purchasing decisions and consumer behavior".

Faced with an increasingly competitive market, the brand is no longer the only parameter for the quality of the product or service. Years ago, the brand was just an identification, term, sign, symbol, a resource used to differentiate a company, a manufacturer from another. Today, it takes a lot more than identification. It is also necessary to focus on competition, especially on direct competition. Let's see!

Figure 2.4

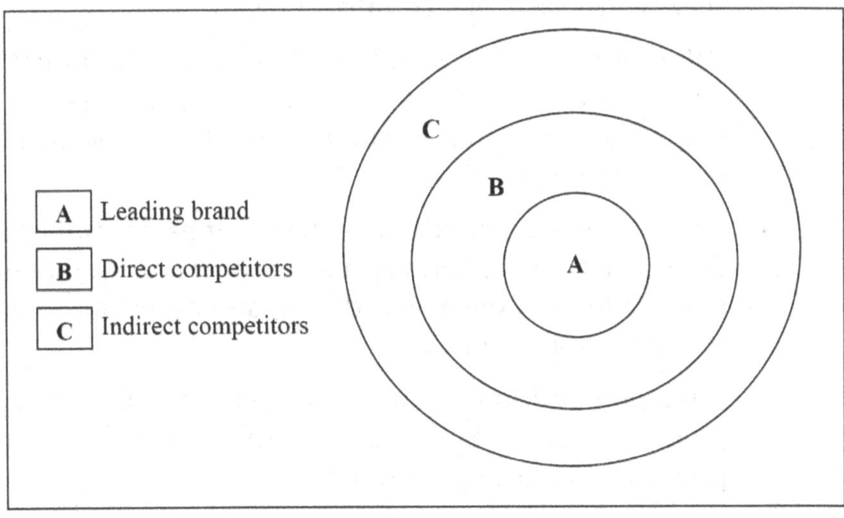

Data source: Global Consulting

The model above represents the level of competition that typically defines market share. In the center is the leading brand represented by the letter *A*. Then, direct competition represented by the letter *B*. The letter *C* therefore represents indirect competition. This entire process directly involves the concept of marketing. For this reason, we can say that marketing works as a system in which all components have relationships with each other. Today, more and more indirect competitors are becoming direct, because of communication. The global market is more competitive, with closer or substitute products and services. Each sector is made up of several competing products, all trying to gain market share.

An industry means a group of companies that offer a product or a category of products. Sectors are classified according to the number of suppliers, levels of product differentiation and the presence or absence of barriers, entry, exit or degree of vertical or global integration.

The starting point for differentiating an industry is the number of suppliers or companies operating in it, or whether the product is homogeneous or heterogeneous. These characteristics give rise to four types of sectoral structure. Let's see!

- **Monopoly** - Only one company provides a product or service in a particular country or region.
- **Oligopoly** - Only a small number of companies provide a product or service in a particular country or region. The oligopoly is made up of companies whose objective is to produce commodities.
- **Monopolistic competition** - Many competitors are able to differentiate their offerings in whole or in part. Competitors are able to meet the needs, desires and expectations of the market in a superior way.
- **Pure competition** - Many competitors offer the same product or service. Since there is no basis for differentiation, prices are practically the same.

Competitors are companies that serve the same needs as consumers. From the moment a company starts to identify its competitors, it must also identify its positioning, as well as its strengths and weaknesses. The company also needs to consider external factors that are uncontrollable, but that influence purchasing decisions or consumer behavior.

Every industry contains good and bad competitors. The good ones are those that act according to the rules of the sector and establish prices compatible with the segment. Bad competitors try to buy market share rather than conquer it. Companies typically compete with others that are in the same market position, and those that rank second and third are known as challengers or followers. These companies usually adopt different measures, but they have the same objective, namely, to increase market share. On the other hand, brand management does a lot to limit competition. It is often the only factor capable of overcoming direct competition. The brand is the only factor capable of crossing borders! Hence the reason for the concept of a [2]market without borders. With the growing advancement of the digital platform, the borderless

2 The digital platform created the borderless market, where the biggest challenge will be to conquer the consumer's purchasing preferences. In this market, location or geography does not matter, as technology has no borders.

market has been standing out for its strong presence in almost every country in the world.

On the other hand, many companies prefer to follow the market leader rather than challenge it, as they will not have to bear the costs of research, development and innovation. Thus, companies avoid stealing customers from each other. Instead, they feature similar offerings almost always following the market leader.

There are three measures that are normally taken by direct competition!

Counterfeiting - Exact copy of the leader's product, however, without quality and reference in the consumer market.

Cloning - Imitation of the product, however, with the same quality and market reference. It is important to remember that this measure can lead to endless lawsuits in court, especially when the product is patented or licensed.

Imitation - As the name says, it is an imitation. The difference is basically in the price, relatively low compared to the leading brand in the market. China is a classic example of this type of market.

These are measures adopted by the competition, but they exert a strong influence on consumer behavior. However, some of these measures can lead to legal proceedings. For this reason, it is critical to create significant differences in the minds of the consumer or customer.

GENERAL THEORY OF SYSTEMS

Systems theory is a thought capable of providing basic conditions for the integration of organizational theories. General systems theory emerged in 1950 from the research of German biologist Ludwig Von Bertalanffy. TGS is based on three basic premises. Let's see!

1) Systems exist within systems.

2) Systems are open.

3) The functions of a system depend on its structure.

Systems theory allows us to better understand phenomena within a general perspective, allowing for the interrelationship and integration of subjects, which are most often of different natures. The system can be understood as the set of parts put together that form the whole or the system.

There are different types of systems, which can be differentiated as to their constitution and nature.

Constitution

Physical systems (machines, equipment, objects...). Abstract systems (ideas, concepts, hypotheses...).

Nature

Closed systems (does not exchange energy or information with the environment, and does not influence it).

Open systems (interacting with the environment, exchanging information, undergoing changes, adjusting and adapting to survive the influences of the environment).

COMPONENTS AND CHARACTERISTICS OF A SYSTEM

Inputs

Material, human, financial and technological resources.

Processing

Processing means that all inputs or raw materials will be processed.

Departures

Output means the transformation of raw material into finished product.

Entropy

It is the tendency that organisms have to break down. Closed physical systems are subject to the force of entropy (disorder of the system). One example is the machine, which tends to deteriorate through use. However, in the open biological or social system, entropy can be interrupted, turning into what we call negative entropy or homeostasis.

Homeostasis

It's the opposite of entropy. In the human organism, the homeostatic process is automatically present whenever there is a disturbance in the system. Thus, whenever a factor, cause or circumstance affects the system, the body tends to generate antibodies, in order to rebalance the system. In organizations, the homeostatic process does not have the same mechanism, as it is not automatic. It is essential that the company develop mechanisms to keep the system in balance.

Feedback

It is the system's ability to keep itself balanced against what has already happened. The open system organization operates in a given environment in constant interaction. Therefore, it is necessary for the organization to have control mechanisms to maintain or change its future state or performance.

As a starting point, we will use systems theory to illustrate how the brand undergoes the production and transformation processes of the product. Let's see!

Figure 2.5

Systems theory

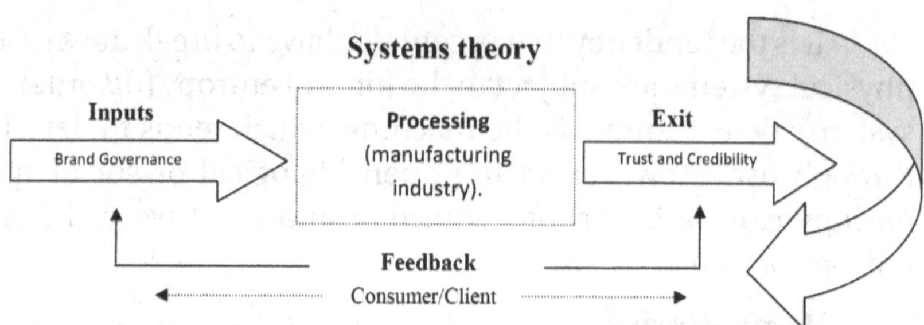

Analyzing the figure, we can see how systems theory collaborates perfectly with brand management. Brand governance starts exactly in the transformation processes, that is, transformation of raw material into finished product. The brand undergoes this process and the result or output is also the brand's trust and credibility. The Feedback is the mental status of the entire process of producing and transforming the product. Obviously, the higher the mental statuses, the greater will be the brand's trust and credibility in the market.

TOTAL QUALITY

Total quality is a multidisciplinary management technique that uses several tools and productive methods of a company. The concept of total quality means seeking the satisfaction of all agents involved in the production and transformation process of the product or service. The objective of total quality is the satisfaction of all people who have some participation in the production process.

PRINCIPLES OF TOTAL QUALITY

Customer Satisfaction

When thinking about total quality, customers are seen as the most important part of the corporate brand. Therefore, customer service actions, partnerships and also surpassing expectations must be created. An organization must direct the marketing plan, through the satisfaction of the target market. It is important to know the opinion about the services provided so that the marketing plan can be used to improve your actions. With this analysis, it is possible to know the answer to the changes that are constantly taking place in the market.

Participatory Management

Companies must get used to passing on information to employees, as this mobilization process generates more competitiveness in the company. It should also encourage employees to participate in decisions and share information. Creativity must be used to solve problems, and managers must lead their teams without restricting human potential. Leadership must listen, motivate, delegate, inform, share and transform knowledge into a solution.

Improvement of Human Resources

It is necessary to value the human element, motivating the employee in the work environment. Humans are an essential part of a productive process, and motivating them helps to increase potential and initiative in the workplace.

Continuous Improvement

The company must anticipate consumer or customer expectations with innovation, use new technologies and use performance indicators. Improvement must be a premise within the company. Better assess your actions and processes, your performance in relation to the competition, take on new challenges and be open and receptive to new technologies and market trends.

Delegation of power

The control of a company becomes more efficient when responsibility is divided and decisions have autonomy. An entrepreneur cannot see and do everything within a company. Thus, delegating powers is the best option, reducing barriers and delays in solving problems. Decisions made must comply with company policies and standards. Delegating and being delegated requires responsibility, commitment and leadership.

Disseminate Information

Information must flow in the company as best as possible. Establish an internal information system and keep the flow going with great transparency. Objectives must be achieved with the commitment of everyone in the company. It is important to inform consumers and customers about the company's corporate mission and objectives, ensuring greater transparency and participation in the competition.

Do not accept errors

The policy in a company should be *zero defect or failure*, and it should be adopted by all segments of a company. Corrective actions must be introduced in recurrent cases *(recalls)*, as preventing an error is cheaper than fixing it in the future. Remembering that partnerships can also cause failures due to products with a manufacturing defect of origin. In this case, brand positioning is potentially affected due to flaws in the corporate system or manufacturing defect.

THEORY OF HUMAN NEEDS

The theory of human needs or hierarchy of human needs was developed by American psychologist Abraham H. Maslow. According to Maslow, man is motivated by a hierarchy or scale of needs. Maslow conceptually summarized the theory of human needs, structured on five different levels. Let's see!

Figure 2.6

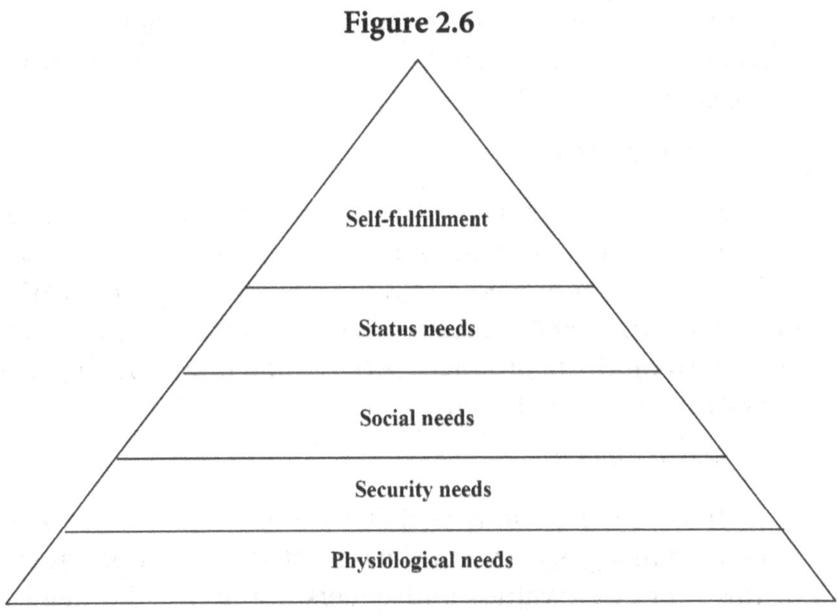

Data source: author's collection

According to the figure, we have five different levels of needs. From now on, we'll look at each of Maslow's needs and what that could mean for the manufacturing industry.

Physiological Needs

Man is a being endowed with needs, as soon as one of his needs is satisfied, soon another appears in its place. This process is continuous from birth to death. Human needs are organized into a series of levels or hierarchy of value. At the lowest level, but of great importance when not satisfied, are physiological needs. Unmet need does not motivate behavior. Remembering that physiological needs must be satisfied by any environment. Therefore, it is not directly related to brand management or governance.

Security Needs

What is called security need are protection needs, especially considering the diversity of products and services in the global market. When the consumer or customer trusts the brand, they are more than willing to take risks. However, when you feel threatened, the chances of risk increase. Therefore, the safety factor must be considered a basic need to be satisfied by any product or service in the consumer market.

Social needs

Social needs are actually status needs. Mental status reveals society's need to maintain brand values and beliefs. The need for self-esteem or improved quality of life shows quite clearly how important social needs are. It is in this hierarchy of needs that the absolute majority of products, services and brands in Brazil and in the world are concentrated.

Status Needs

The need for status is that placed above the social needs of man. Status goes beyond the expectations of modern society! In this hierarchy, values and beliefs are above the needs they represent, self-esteem and improved quality of life. The luxury market represents these needs well and, consequently, the needs of a specific group of consumers.

Need for Self-Realization

Self-fulfillment is an absolute necessity, that is, few people in the world have access to this human need. Self-fulfillment is a multi-billion dollar market, so few people have access to this billion dollar market.

LEADERSHIP IN ORGANIZATIONS

Leadership in organizations is an extremely relevant subject, especially considering the importance of the digital platform in the modern economy. We can understand leadership as a process to motivate and shape other people's behavior. Leadership takes place in a variety of settings and forms. Before we discuss the various forms of leadership, let's draw a distinction between leadership and management.

Leadership and administration are similar in some respects, but different in others. It is possible to be a leader without necessarily being a manager and the reverse is true. The bases of power used by leaders and managers tend to be different. Managers can direct the efforts of others because of their formal organizational power. If a department head asks an employee to do such a thing, and the person does exactly what was mentioned, that head is probably being a manager. On the other hand, a leader does not need to resort to a formal position to influence a subordinate.

Challenge and leadership

When it comes to challenges, leaders must be ready to take responsibility above all else. For the most part, any leader's success depends on his ability to handle and overcome challenges. There are some types of leadership that we can highlight. Charismatic leader, executive leader, coercive (authoritarian) leader and educational leader. Let's see!

Charismatic leader - He is the one who inspires his followers to trust, credibility, spontaneous acceptance and emotional involvement. The charismatic leader is seen by his followers as someone who has an exceptional maturity or quality.

Executive leader - It is the one who emerged due to the moral and ethical order. He has various skills and competencies within the organization.

Authoritarian leader - Is one who exercises leadership, through coercion, which can be verbal or physical.

Educational leader - He is the one who usually sets an example, his team members have a responsible relationship with their work.

POWER AND LEADERSHIP

There is no leadership without power and autonomy!

There are five basic types of power. Legitimate, rewarding, coercive, specialization and referral power. Let's see!

Legitimate power - It is the power created and transmitted by the organization. The person (manager) in charge of a group in general can tell their team how to carry out their tasks and so on.

Reward power - Typical company rewards include, for example, salary increases, benefits, career path, etc. The greater the reward power, the greater the corporate brand recognition.

Coercive power - It is the power to impose submission. In some environments coercion can take the form of force. The more punitive elements a person can sustain, the more coercive power he will have.

Power of Specialization - It is the power based on knowledge and wisdom. A manager must know the best way to lead. The more important the knowledge and the smaller the number of people who hold it, the more expert power the manager will have.

Power of relevance - It is based on the leader and his or her qualities. The followers tend to look like him, as they admire the way they manage to lead.

Important tip:

Italian football player, Marco **Verratti**, is a big name in the global market. *Verratti* is a sophisticated name that represents well men's fashion, perfumery, cosmetics, automotive, sports and nautical markets. Verratti is a timeless name that represents well the segment where self-esteem and personal fulfillment are the center of attention.

CHAPTER 3
BRANDING SERVICE

What is McDonald's business? Product or Service?

The service sector is considered the fuel of the global economy. According to Kotler and Keller (2006), the service is everything that one party transfers to another, and that does not result in ownership of anything. However, it is necessary to professionalize the service, that is, transform the human element into human capital, as the service is linked to the performance of the human element.

As there is no transfer or ownership rights, the image and credibility of the service are the only essentially tangible factors for the consumer or customer. Transforming the product into a service requires knowledge, and above all, professional qualification. It is noteworthy that technology is an important factor, but it is only a supporting role between the brand and the final consumer. However, in the service, brand management is crucial, because there is almost always no basis for differentiation other than the company's commercial name. Thus, creating differences is fundamental, especially with regard to the image and performance of the service. For this reason, every service needs its own identity, identification and characteristics.

Often, the entrepreneur does not know or is not aware of the true motivation of his business. Thus, the greater the value of the product or service, the less direct and personal involvement with the human element will be. However, the lower the value of the product or service, the greater the direct and personal involvement with the human element. We can imagine, for example, that the McDonald's business is a product, but based on the value of the product, the service becomes the great highlight and competitive differential. In other words, we can say that every service assumes a prominent position, since the value of the product does not influence consumer behavior.

We develop a model regarding the processes and exchange relationships with the consumer or customer. Therefore, it is an indispensable strategic analysis tool in any service operation. This model was developed to represent a very interesting theory, mainly from the point of view of the target market, that is, from outside the organization. Let's see!

Figure 3.1

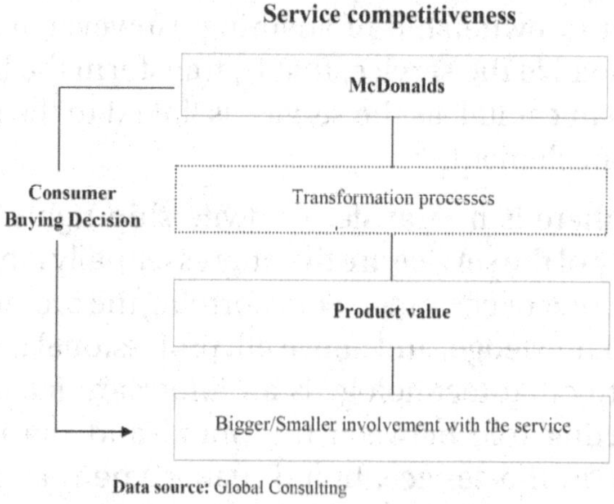

Data source: Global Consulting

Looking at the figure, we come to the conclusion that the value of the product or service has a direct influence on consumer purchase decisions. So the greater or lesser the value of the product, the greater or lesser will be the involvement of the human element with the service. It is also noteworthy that the higher the level of demand, the greater the variability of the service. For this reason, it is essential to verify the environment's carrying capacity and whether the service offer is compatible with the level of demand.

With the growing digital environment, the service has become technological, electronic and digital. The [3]face-to-face

3 Face-to-face service is essentially characterized by human participation or presence.

service (SP) has been losing space in the face of information technology. As a result, the [4]distance service (SAD) has been growing rapidly in the global market. The [5]electronic service (SE), that is, performed basically by machines, has a huge significance in the consumer market, as it is practical, safe and reliable. The service landscape has dramatically changed consumer behavior. The logic of consumption is anchored in technology. Google Andriod, for example, can be considered the forerunner of the digital environment. The Android generation is connected 24 hours a day! Smartphone is, without a doubt, the most used electronic device in the world. The world is summed up on a Smartphone! No matter the geography! It's a global trend and it doesn't matter the brand, as Google Android is unaware of the economic nature of any product or service in the global market.

It's basically a blind spot! We can say that Google Andriod is available in the electronic, digital market, as it is very reliable and secure. The competition is not on Google Android, but on the consumer's mental status. Let's see!

Figure 3.2

Brand positioning

Data source: Global Consulting

Analyzing the picture, it is crucial to understand the consumer's level of perception in relation to the brand. Each brand has a special meaning, however, the modern brand, that

4 Concept developed to designate the service model, without the effective human presence or participation. This service is essentially characterized by the digital platform (application).

5 Self-service or electronic service is essentially characterized by machines, without effective human participation.

is, the brand that represents the current market, compared to more traditional brands, tends to be more competitive. For example, the **Xiaomi** brand represents the current market well, compared to the **Apple** brand. Analyzing the brand's lifecycle, we realize that the Xiaomi brand is more current and modern. This is normal? Yes! It's up to the Apple brand to be more competitive and contemporary. Quality is fundamental, but it is not the only factor capable of motivating consumer behavior. The brand needs to be current and modern. Traditional brands need to show competitiveness against the Chinese brand Xiaomi. Technology and transformation brands need to strengthen the consumer's memory whenever competition emerges as a motivating factor for human behavior.

In this context, the author also developed a professional qualification program, [6]*Human Professional Service (HPS)*, specific for the service sector. The objective of the program is the professional qualification, in view of the needs, desires and trends of the services market. This means that the workforce needs to conform to market expectations. Despite the stratospheric growth of the digital environment, the human element is still the forerunner of the service sector, as technology lacks the feeling, emotion and capacity to understand the complexity of human nature. With the growth of the distance service (SAD) the human element has been losing visibility in the services market. The internet, for example, is a market without borders and, essentially, digital. An environment where the human element becomes just a supporting role in the face of the predominance of technology.

What is the future of humanity? Will the human element be replaced by machines? Are we facing the suppression of man, facing technology? Let's analyze the behavior of technology in the face of the growing digital environment. Technology also needs maintenance, governance and management. Let's see!

---

6 Program developed by the author, whose objective is to guide the conduct and management of the service sector in Brazil and worldwide.

Figure 3.3

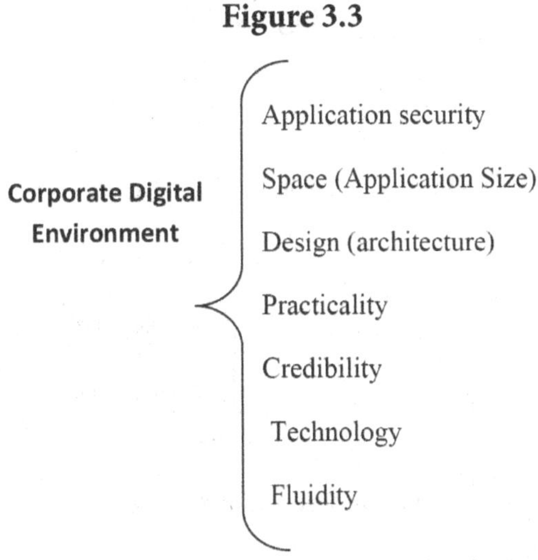

Data source: author's collection

Analyzing the figure, we realize that despite the digital environment, it is necessary to invest in quality, that is, environmental management, security, architecture, credibility, technology and application fluidity. It is extremely important that the application does not crash, be fluid and practical. This concept is also valid for ATMs and self-service. However, the digital environment must expand not only the offer of services, but also that these same services can be replicated in different platforms and market segments.

However, it is necessary to develop measures to control and improve the system or modal of services. If it is in person (SP) the company must offer professional qualification courses, that is, model and improve the face-to-face service. With regard to customer feedback, when the service is essentially face-to-face, a satisfaction survey should be adopted, which can suggest improvement in the performance and execution of the service. Let's see!

Figure 3.4

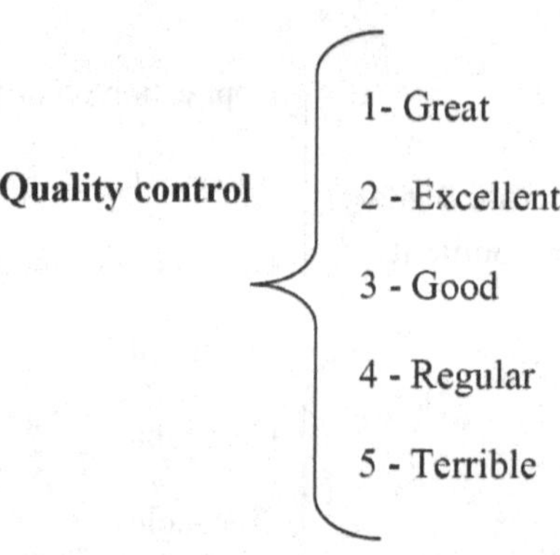

Data source: author's collection

Analyzing the figure, we came to the conclusion that this is a very simple survey and that it can be carried out approximately every 6 months. Give a grade from 0 to 5 for the following question.

Ask the customer! How would you rate our service?

Grades 5 and 4 mean that the service is completely non-existent, that is, superficial and without human warmth. In this case, professional qualification is extremely necessary. Grades 3 and 2 mean that the service are compatible with the needs and expectations of the consumer market. In this case, the research must be carried out only to feed the system or modal of services. A top (excellent) rating means the service is beyond the customer's expectations. In this case, the high value added to the product is also a prominent factor in the market. Remembering that the survey can also be carried out via the internet or digital platform.

However, there is a basic issue in the service sector. The price of the service! How much is a service worth? This question depends on the size of the value added to the product. Let's see!

Figure 3.5

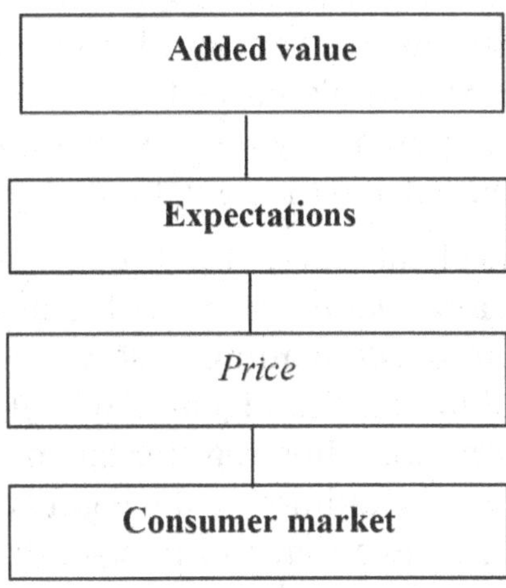

Data source: author's collection

The figure above means that the value added to the product is crucial for the service to be described in an essential way to the product. The final value of the product determines the quality of the service. Therefore, the expectation is regarding the final value of the product. The higher the final value, the greater will be the customer's expectation regarding the quality of the service.

Imagine the customer having the option to check-in on board the aircraft. The customer can make the reservation and make payment when on board the plane [7]**(On Board Pay)**. This means that the system or application can accommodate passengers who have already made the reservation and payment, but also those passengers who prefer to pay at the time of boarding. However, it is necessary to take into account the cargo and logistics capacity of the airport and airlines. Of course, it is just a concept, but in the future it may be a solution, considering the growing advancement of the digital environment. Confirmation of payment by the airline would be instantaneous. Boarding fee, proof of payment, taxation, checklist, etc. All in real time! Certainly, the passenger who opts

7 It is a global concept where the passenger has the option to make a reservation and make payment upon boarding. The service is offered through the digital platform with the effective participation of airlines and also tourism and public security agencies and institutions of each member country of the system or organization.

for the service runs the risk of not finding any more seats available on the aircraft. In this case, the application or system pre-checks and updates customer data and availability of seats on the aircraft. If there is no longer availability, the reservation is automatically cancelled. The option of payment at the time of boarding, avoids both reimbursement and the need to reschedule the trip.

As a control measure, the airline may adopt a payment period hours before take-off, also considering the airlift. Ex: Up to 6 hours before take-off, depending on service availability. Customer registration is done on the digital platform, through biometrics or facial recognition. After registering in the application, the customer receives, in addition to the login and password, a global (universal) access code that can be used by airlines worldwide. Thus, anywhere in the world, the customer no longer needs to check-in, as all information is available on the digital platform. Just make a reservation and monitor service availability.

Therefore, there is no need for airline services at airports, as everything is done on the digital platform. When boarding, just present the global access code at the self-service terminals at airports and make facial recognition. Subsequently, the system verifies the authenticity of the customer's registration before the control and security agencies at the airports. Through the application, the customer can choose the language of origin or destination, to facilitate the simultaneous translation of information between airlines.

Of course, we already have a system, app or something similar on the market. The concept of payment on board is universal, modern and contemporary. The face-to-face service (SP) takes place on board the aircraft or when requested in advance by the customer at airport self-service terminals. The international passport follows the same line of thought, that is, a universal code for each passenger. Another important feature is that the system can be used as a control, protection and prevention measure in the event of a **pandemic** or **endemic** disease. The system can easily block the flow of passengers at airport self-service terminals.

As for the platform, companies interested in offering the service need authorization from the tourism and public security bodies and institutions of each member country of the system or organization. In terms of platform technology companies can easily offer a reliable service platform. Ex: *Google, Microsoft, Starlink, Meta platform, TikTok etc.*The user has the option to search the platform and choose the best onboard service options. Remember that the global access code acts as a kind of global identity for the passenger. In other words, it's the passenger's birth certificate. Registration can be done normally; just follow the instructions on the platform.

INTANGIBILITY SCALE

Figure 3.6

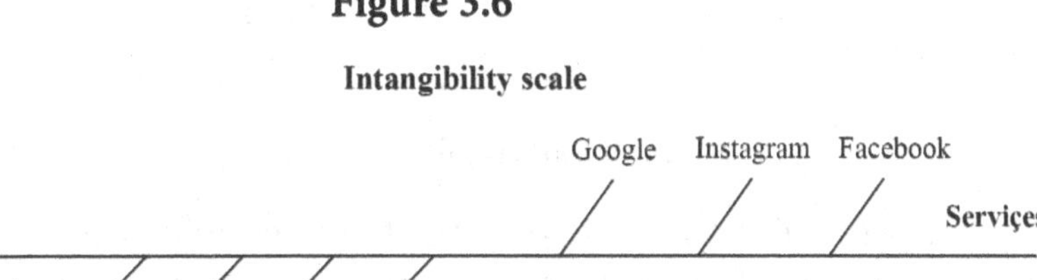

data source: author's collection

Looking at the figure above, we can see that it is not always easy to identify a product or service. Often, the business philosophy or reason starts from the moment the entrepreneur correctly identifies the influence of the product or service on the consumer's daily life. This is increasingly important in any business platform. Therefore, the service model is the most suitable, as it values the human element and, therefore, the expectations of the consumer or customer.

Another important feature in the service sector is related to the present and future purchase stage of the consumer. The service can be purchased, however, there is no logical sequence between purchase and use of the service. In other words, this means that the present stage is different from the future stage of services. Let's see!

Figure 3.7

Present and future stage of services

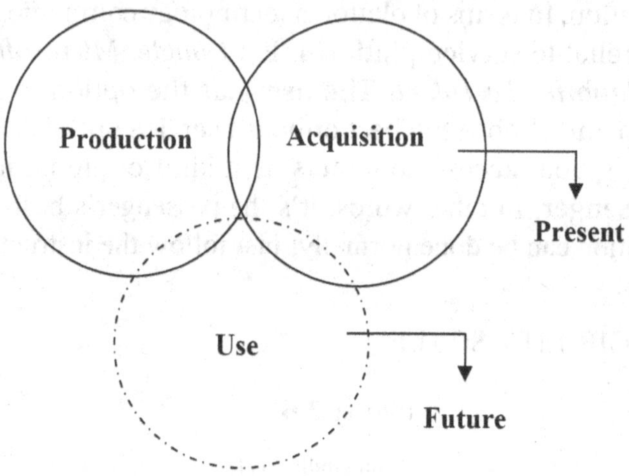

Data source: Global Consulting

Based on the figure, we come to the conclusion that, despite having purchasing and decision-making power, the consumer cannot exactly determine the use of the services, even though it is available in the consumer market. Therefore, we cannot accurately determine the present and future status of the services. On the other hand, it is necessary to be very careful with services contracted in the short term, and used in the long term. The consumer needs tangible elements that can demonstrate the quality and efficiency of the service also in the long term.

SERVICE CHARACTERISTICS

The service characteristics are extremely important, as they prioritize the needs, desires and expectations of the consumer or customer. These characteristics are related to the offer of services, and how they can be decisive in the process of buying or choosing a brand. Let's see!

Intangibility - Means absence of property or matter.

Inseparability - Meaning that it is not possible to separate the consumer or customer from the service environment.

Variability - Means that the service can vary depending on demand, that is, the greater the demand, the greater the variability of the service. However, the variability also concerns competition in the market. This means that the same service is available. In this case, there is no way to differentiate one service from another, except for the quality of service and brand positioning in the market.

Perishability - Means that the service is perishable when not used. This feature of the service is also seasonal, that is, it can vary according to the season or seasons of the year. A classic example is Disney! The offer of services may vary depending on demand availability.

According to the characteristics, it is necessary to make the service tangible, visible to the consumer or customer. Even though the service has not yet been performed, the consumer or customer needs evidence that can influence their decision when purchasing and using the service. A classic example is airlines. *Ex: American Airlines, Etihad Airways, Emirates etc.*

Brand positioning and image can influence the consumer's purchase decision. However, managing evidence is extremely important to prevent service failures. Despite the gigantic growth of the digital environment, inseparability is a treacherous characteristic, as it is directly related to the performance of the human element, as well as the environment where the face-to-face service will be performed.

The professionalization of the face-to-face (SP) or digital (SAD) service is an extremely competitive factor. We cannot imagine that it is possible to offer a poor quality service without damaging the image of the service brand. Tourism, for example, necessarily depends on the quality of the service.

Service variability is another feature that has a huge influence on consumer behavior or purchasing decisions. Variability is usually influenced by the level of demand, that is, the greater the demand, the greater the variability of the service. As mentioned above, variability also concerns the level of market competition.

SERVICE QUALITY MANAGEMENT

Based on customer satisfaction, we have developed a management model that values both the use of technology and the satisfaction of the service professional. The human element plays a crucial role in the professionalization of the service, but not everyone is able to provide a good service. The professional's profile can help a lot, considering that the smile on the face, the desire to serve and the satisfaction of being with people are important ingredients for hiring a good service professional. This can also mean an important competitive advantage, as the service professional's performance reflects the brand's commitment to providing a high standard of service.

The model basically serves the face-to-face service (SP). Let's see!

Figure 3.8

Service quality management

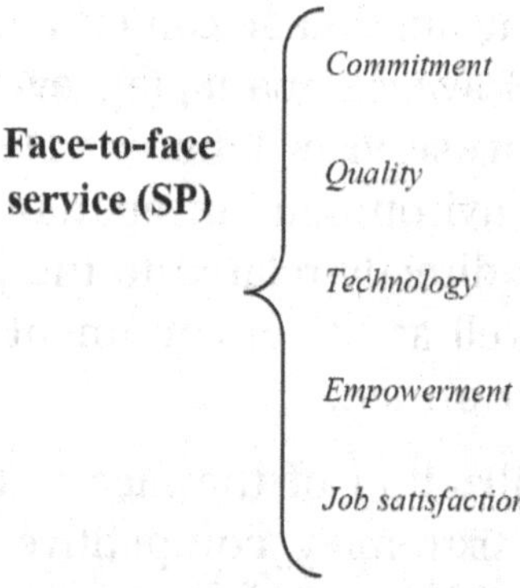

Data source: Global Consulting

Some tools can greatly influence the professionalization of the service and labor specialization. Let's see!

Commitment - More important than providing a good service is being committed to it, that is, commitment helps to characterize and identify the service. Therefore, it is essential to establish a quality standard, especially with regard to service. It is essential to establish a deadline for the customer to have a quick response in case of service failure.

Quality - Quality is inherent to everything that concerns the product or service. However, we need to be aware that the value of the product is usually related to the transformation processes and not necessarily the quality of service. In this way, the value of the service is related to the final value of the product. On the other hand, the quality of the service must not vary due to price or added value.

Technology - The use of technology is essential! However, we need to be aware that technology is only one component between the company and the consumer. Under no circumstances can technology be considered a protagonist or main character. As stated before, technology has no feeling, emotion and, therefore, there is no loyalty on the part of the consumer or customer. Unfortunately, the digital platform has drastically reduced the interaction of the human element in the service sector. However, the human element continues to be the protagonist of the face-to-face service.

Empowerment - This tool is extremely important, as the service professional needs power and autonomy to solve any problems with the execution of the service. Remember, the consumer or customer cannot be on the sidelines of an unsolved problem. It is crucial to empower service professionals! Subsequently, the service professional needs to be empathetic, that is, be able to put himself in the shoes of the consumer or customer, especially taking into account the variability of the service and the level (displacement) of demand in the market.

Professional Satisfaction - A satisfied employee is worth a thousand! This concept can help a lot to understand the importance of the word satisfaction. A disgruntled employee is like a terrorist! Causes irreparable damage and loss! In this way, employee satisfaction becomes an extremely important tool in any company, agency or service institution.

SERVICE MANAGEMENT MODEL

This model is practically the structural basis of any service in the consumer market. Let's see!

Figure 3.9

Service management model

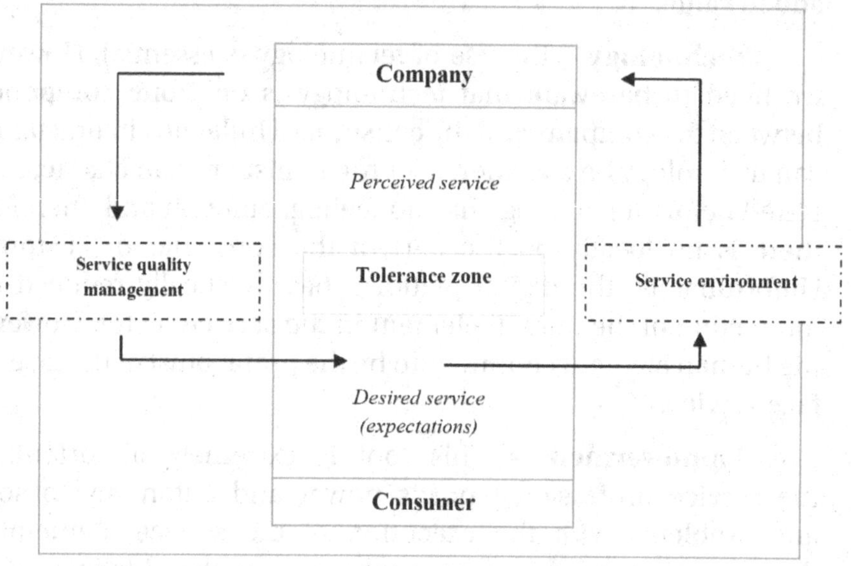

Data source: Global Consulting

Looking closely at the figure, we can see that the structural basis of the service includes aspects of management and quality management, prioritizing the service environment. The consumer or customer is usually in the tolerance zone. This means to say that the consumer is not satisfied with the service, but manages to tolerate it for some time. Note that at the ends we have the company on one side and the consumer on the other. Traditionally, every customer is a consumer, so it is essential to win over the consumer on the first purchase. This means that first impressions are important in the service environment.

POSITIONING AND IMAGE OF THE SERVICE BRAND

Years ago, the emphasis was only on marketing and product or service segmentation. Today we can say, with certainty, that the emphasis is on brand positioning. Positioning refers to the image and credibility of the brand in the mind of the consumer or customer. The brand occupies a privileged space in the consumer's mind! However, we need to be aware that it takes years to conquer a space in the consumer's mind, and it only takes a few seconds to completely destroy everything that has been conquered. For this reason, brand positioning is not just about the product, but also about the brand's relationship with the consumer.

In the services sector, positioning occupies a larger space, as it is something intangible. There is a line of thought that according to the author, the brand's positioning is on *stand by*. This mainly means that the brand is vulnerable to the quality of service. In this case, this thought also reflects the urgent need to apply this concept to the manufacturing industry, as it is practically impossible to offer a good product without necessarily also offering a good service. The [8]stand by concept in the service sector serves to illustrate the importance of exceeding consumer expectations. For this reason, the service sector must adopt this concept, as the service exerts a strong influence on the image and positioning of the brand. Let's see!

8 Concept developed by the author to illustrate consumer behavior in relation to service quality. In this case, the consumer is in standby mode, awaiting the operation and execution of the service to check the quality in relation to the image and positioning of the corporate brand.

Figure 3.10

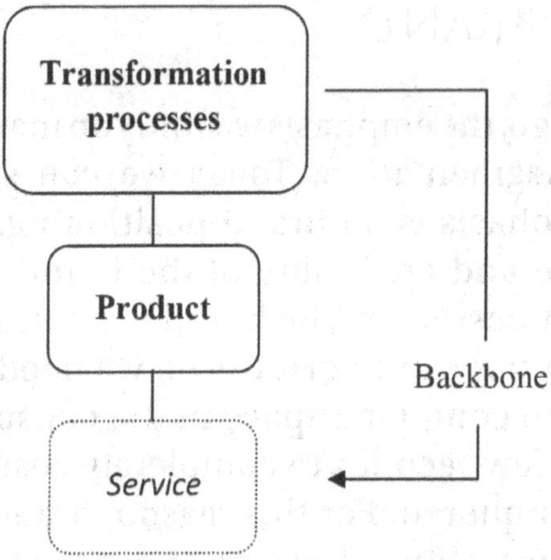

Data source: Global Consulting

Based on the figure, we see that service is the backbone of any product in the consumer market. The service is present in the transformation industry and, essentially, in the tertiary sector. Combining the transformation industry with the service industry, we have a stratospheric market of opportunities. For that, we just need to offer a quality service. After considering positioning, we must consider the market and segmentation of the product or service. In addition, it is necessary to establish a service model, always prioritizing the human element, considering the characteristics of the service, digital platform and brand longevity. Remembering that one service cannot be exactly the same as another. The similarity, imitation of products in the market is quite common, however, this rule does not apply to the services market. Although many service companies look a lot like each other, the service is usually personalized or customized, according to the needs, desires and expectations of the consumer market.

The market needs to be well segmented, taking into account the price range as an important index in the operation or execution of the service. It is possible to segment the market according to age, gender, income, lifestyle, education level or social class. Considering the market, segmentation and positioning, the image becomes a competitive advantage of the company, institution or franchise. The image reflects the brand's excellent positioning in the market. Therefore, this tool becomes essential in the face of modern marketing trends. It doesn't matter if we are in the digital or global world. It is crucial to develop a service model that is compatible with the consumer's needs, desires and expectations. Customizing the service is essential, especially when the service takes place in person.

DISTRIBUTION OF SERVICES

The location and classification of services are extremely important factors, close to what is actually possible to offer the market. The distribution of services can help us a lot to understand how each service works, especially considering the geographic location. Let's see!

Figure 3.11

Classification and Location of Services

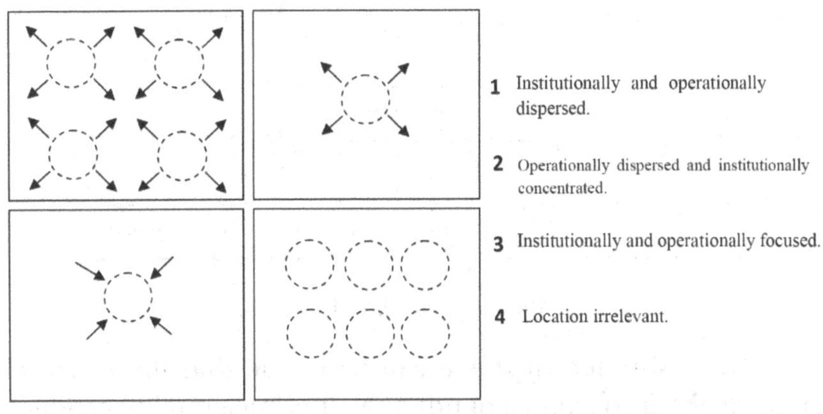

Data source: author's collection

Based on the figure, we see that geographic location exerts a strong influence on the operation of any service. The chains of stores, franchises and dealerships, for example, are institutionally and operationally dispersed. Consulting firms, for example, are operationally dispersed but institutionally concentrated.

Hospitals, for example, are institutionally and operationally concentrated. Irrelevant location is the one that allows the consumer or customer to meet the service. Ex: *Disney*

SERVICE LOGISTICS

Logistics is an increasingly important factor in the modern economy. In the digital world, where practicality is crucial in any company, service logistics plays a strategic and competitive role in the market. Consumption on the internet is increasing due to the digital platform. Direct marketing is only possible thanks to a set of services such as technology, communication and transport. Let's see!

Figure 3.12

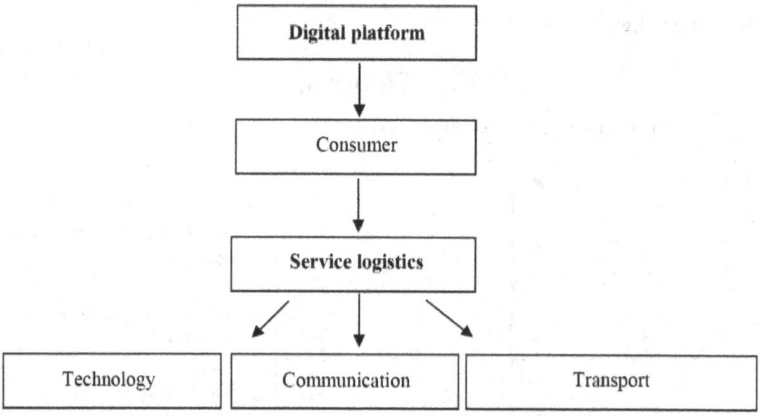

Data source: Global Consulting

In a simpler view, we can conclude that the figure above reflects the importance of not only offering a quality product, but also a quality service. This concept reflects the importance of the digital environment and effectively refers us to the market without borders. Obviously, we are talking about large companies, but the market space has been drastically changing the reality of the consumer market. Today the partnership has become a billionaire business! The digital platform is the driving force behind this corporate market that drives the services sector. Let's see!

Figure 3.13

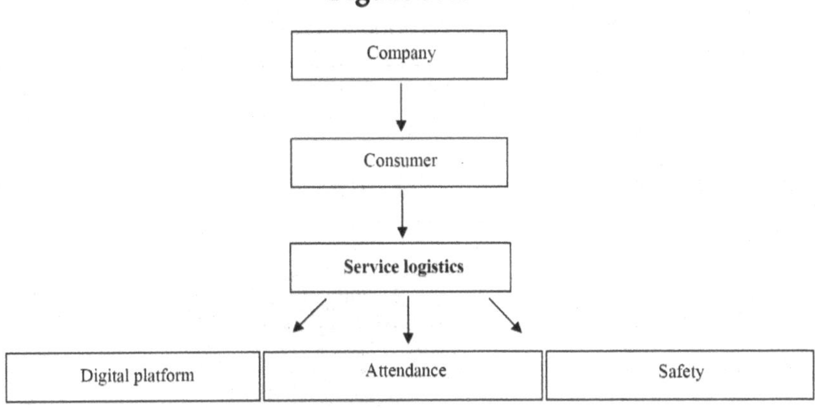

Data source: Global Consulting

Analyzing the scheme, we realize how much logistics is essential in the service environment. Therefore, the quality and efficiency of the service cannot vary, especially considering the consumer's tolerance zone. Thus, service logistics is as important as choosing a product or service on the internet. If the service is not satisfactory, obviously, the consumer will change service and, therefore, sales channel. Therefore, it is necessary to offer maximum security to the consumer. We will show how the service naturally develops from principles, which in practice reveal the importance of the service environment. Let's see!

Figure 3.14

Seven principles of service

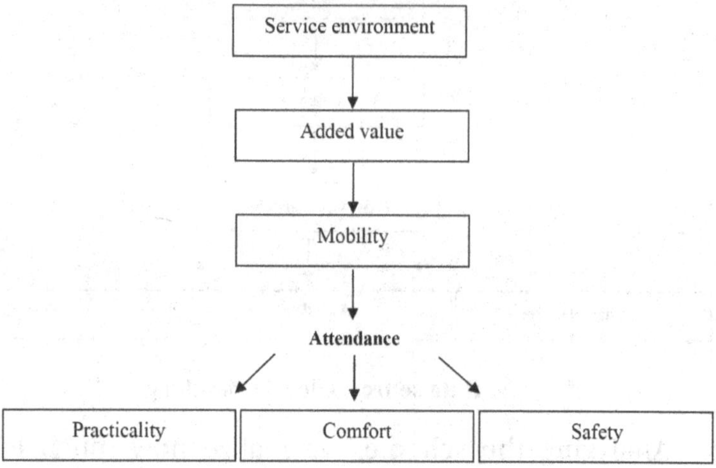

Data source: Global Consulting

According to the schema, we observe [9]seven essential principles of service. This process concerns the logistics of services, that is, how the supply chain of a service works in practice. This concept can help to understand the landscape of the service sector in the consumer market. Let's see!

Service environment: The environment in this case is like an industrial production line. In other words, it's where everything gets done and processed. However, it is also necessary to consider the digital platform as a service environment. The difference lies in the face-to-face service (SP) and the distance service (SAD). Remembering that we also have the electronic service (SE), that is, the service basically performed by self-service machines. However, the face-to-face service must take into account the waiting time for the execution of the service. The longer the waiting time, the greater will be the consumer's dissatisfaction with the service.

Added value: Added value is everything that serves as a basis for positioning the brand's image in the target market. It also serves to make tangible, that is, to make the operation of the

9 Concept developed by the author, whose objective is to understand how the productive and logistical chain of the service sector works.

service tangible or feasible. Can you imagine an airline without an aircraft? A hotel with no means of accommodation? Therefore, the added value assumes the role of segmenting and making the consumer market tangible.

Mobility: Mobility is, without a doubt, a factor that deserves to be highlighted. This means that the consumer is free to choose the product, service, brand that best meets their needs, desires and expectations. The chains of stores, franchises and supermarkets, for example, have a wide range of products. On the other hand, we cannot say the same about the service. This is a fact that deserves to be highlighted in the service sector! However, mobility also concerns the level of competition in the market, that is, the greater the mobility, the greater the impact of competition on the consumer market.

Service/Attendance: Service is everything that concerns the consumer. It is clear that professional qualification is an extremely powerful weapon. It is important to emphasize that the service is linked to the image and positioning of the brand in the market. The face-to-face service reflects the feeling of corporate image and, at the same time, integrates the feeling of belonging to the brand.

Practicality: Practicality is an essential component in any service, especially considering the digital platform. However, we need to be aware that technology is only an adjunct to the service. There is no loyalty to technology! Loyalty is anchored in the image and positioning of the service brand.

Comfort: Comfort is another increasingly important component, especially when it comes to service. As well as location and distribution, comfort in the service environment is essential, as we are unable to provide good service without first making sure that the brand offers the necessary space for the service to be performed. It is critical to understand that service is part performance and part human experience.

Security: Security is the basic premise of any product or service. The consumer or customer needs to be aware of their decisions and choices, especially when purchasing future services.

Security is the passport to credibility and, therefore, exerts a strong influence on consumer buying behavior.

CUSTOMER RELATIONSHIP MANAGEMENT (CRM)

Customer relationship management is another important tool that can help to exceed customer or customer expectations.

Customer relationship management is the management of information about each customer and all points of contact with them. Based on the information, the company can customize the service, as today's customer is more demanding in terms of service and price. It is common for a company to offer less for less services. This business model is, in fact, a shot in the foot, because usually the customer changes services when he realizes that there has been a reduction in the performance of the human element. Some airlines, for example, have tried to cut costs by reducing service provision. Result! There was a drastic drop in the number of passengers due to the reduction in service.

Therefore, customer relationship management serves to support the company's image and credibility in the target market. It is necessary to manage relationships and information within the brand's product and service portfolio. For this reason, it is necessary to create a customer database. Let's see!

Figure 3.15

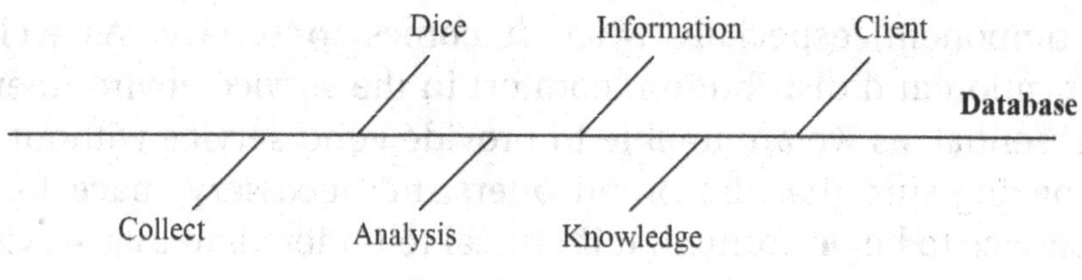

Data source: Global Consulting

A customer database is a comprehensive set of data about current or potential customers. Database is the process of maintaining and using customer data and market information to promote the brand's products and services. It is common for airlines to offer special discounts, for scheduled travel. Of course, there are some cases that are not worth creating a customer database. When customer turnover is very high (public transport) or when the product value unit is very small. In that case, it's not worth creating and maintaining a customer database. On the other hand, the database needs to be secure. Database security is crucial as financial fraud is very common due to customer data leakage. Therefore, digital security is an extremely important marketing tool in the consumer market.

FORMS OF COMMUNICATION IN SERVICES

Communication can greatly help to increase the offer of products and services in the target market. There are some forms of communication that have a strong influence on purchasing decisions or consumer behavior. Let's see!

Exposure - It is one of the most important forms of dissemination, due to the characteristics of the product or service. Exposure allows the consumer to have greater confidence in the product or brand.

Merchandising - It is every effort to present the product or service at the point of sale. Merchandising is very common in series, movies and social networks.

Visual identity program - Image is the public perception of any brand. It is through it that the company informs consumers about products and services. The visual identity program is an important tool, and should be used whenever the company wants to position the product or service in the target market.

As we can clearly see, service exerts a strong influence on purchasing decisions and consumer behavior. This explains the strength of the service sector in the economy, even when there is a right or transfer of ownership. Therefore, we can no longer accept poor quality services, bearing in mind tools to ensure the quality and credibility of the face-to-face service (SP) in Brazil and worldwide.

PROFESSIONAL ETHIC

We are not going to go into the merits of the issue, as the objective is only to draw attention to professional ethics in organizations.

Professional ethics means making the prevailing morality in companies of a specific nationality. However, we urgently need to develop an ethical awareness in terms of economic, social and environmental factors. Ethics can be understood by way of being, character and behavior. We can also say that ethics is the branch of philosophy that seeks to understand society. It is noteworthy that we cannot confuse ethics with jurisprudence. Even though, the law is based on ethical principles. Therefore, Ethics is a set of rules and principles of a given society. It is important to know the difference between ethics and morals. Morals are a set of rules specific to a particular society or civilization. Ethics, therefore, seeks to understand that same society or civilization. The legislation seeks to establish rules for mutual coexistence between people from the same society or organization.

Business ethic

When it comes to business ethics, we imagine a set of rules and values for a particular company. A set of factors such as globalization, economic, environmental, philosophical and religious guidelines. Therefore, business ethics is not just a stage theme or a modern fallacy. There are a set of ethical factors that we need to put into practice. Such factors require ethical leadership and, above all, ethics in people management. Ethical relationship with employees, ethics in hiring, ethics in remaining in the organization and ethics in employee termination. Thus, business ethics cannot be just a political, social, economic or environmental discourse. It is important to remember that business ethics is an extremely important marketing tool, given the transformation industry and the growth of digital technology. In other words, this means that the greater the transformation processes and technology, the greater the ethical and moral responsibility of the corporate brand.

Important tip:

In the services market it is not possible to test the quality before purchasing or using the services. This means that it is not possible to "test-drive" any service operation. On the other hand, self-service can freeze the brand's image and positioning, as the service is essentially electronic (SE). Therefore, this market is subject to commoditization since there is no differentiation between one service and another. The difference is only in the company's trade name. The front office is basically technological and electronic! In this case, only the credibility of the brand has significant real value for the consumer.

Important tip:

Onboard payment system: Initially designed for airlines, the system could also be available for hotels, cruise lines, theme parks, etc. Payment can be made in various ways, using digital currency or any other conventional payment method. Passengers who make multiple reservations and do not use the service will be automatically blocked by the system. All services offered by airlines can be paid on board, offering passengers a real-time experience, as well as personalizing service according to passenger needs. Customizing services on board can reduce travel costs for both passengers and airlines. Finally, the system can also implement various control and security measures. Remembering that we already have an onboard payment system on the market; however, the idea here is to develop a global system (autonomous) where all services are offered through a digital platform (app). The system verifies all services offered by airlines and makes them available on the platform. In person service will also be available at airports and onboard aircraft. Obviously, the system eliminates the need for airline apps, as well as the need for airline counters at airports, as all the information is available in a single system. The system selects the desired airline and provides all the information to passengers and users. Agencies, tour operators, and airlines can offer travel packages and promotions through the platform. Obviously, all services can be paid in advance, including onboard services. The system is divided into three parts! Passengers, system users and system administrators. On longer trips, passengers can decide exactly what they want to consume, including scheduling your meals at specific times.The user has the option to buy the ticket for another person, simply provide the global access code. Finally, in addition to being modern and contemporary, the system is an excellent tool for international security.

CHAPTER 4

BRAND VISUAL COMMUNICATION

We will address the importance of visual communication and its effects on brand positioning. Let's mention why transformation processes have a direct influence on brand positioning. Visual communication is an extremely important tool, especially in the goods industry. For that reason, it needs to be in tune with the brand's values and beliefs. In the manufacturing industry, credibility and trust are exactly in the brand. Thus, it is extremely important to raise awareness of all agents directly involved with the production and transformation processes of the product.

It is noteworthy that the commitment to the brand begins exactly in the transformation processes. Even though this process is not significant for the consumer (blind spot), the brand suffers a contrast, that is, it is extremely significant, because it starts to represent in practice the entire process of transforming the product. Let's see!

Figure 4.1

Manufacturing industry

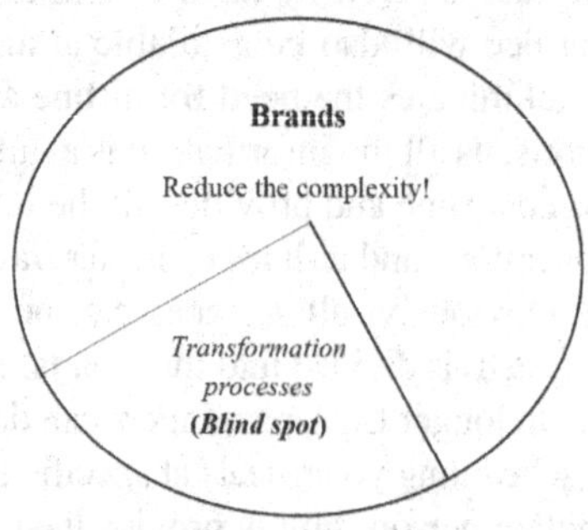

Data source: Global Consulting

Observing the figure, we notice that the production and transformation processes occupy a larger space in the goods industry. This is because there is no direct consumer involvement in the transformation process. Thus, the brand's objective is to reduce complexity, making the entire process effectively under the brand, product or service. On the other hand, it also means that the brand's values and beliefs are rooted in the production processes. These values represent the rational, functional and tangible process of the product. However, these values also represent the emotional, symbolic and intangible process of the brand. The brand concept goes beyond the identification of the product or service, and reinforces the idea that the brand is a set of tangible and intangible values. Let's see!

Figure 4.2

Brand equity features

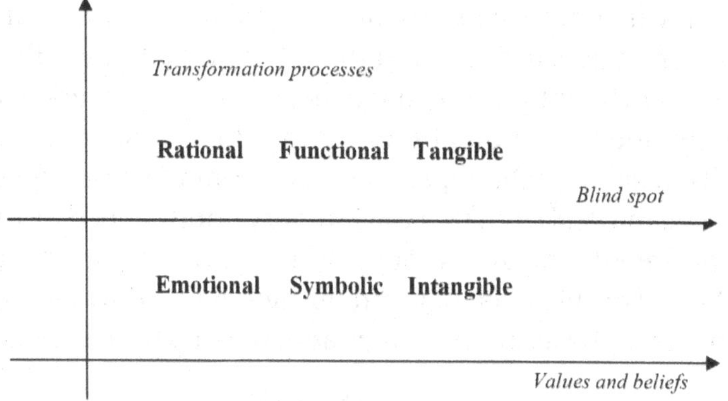

Data source: Global Consulting

According to the figure, tangible values represent the performance of the brand, and intangible values represent the image, appearance and personality of the brand. This thought collaborates directly with the product or service, and refers us to the brand's value. Let's see!

Figure 4.3

Data source: Global Consulting

Looking at the figure, we can better understand the brand's value in the consumer market. We can also understand how the brand is an indicator of trust and credibility. Value indicators reflect how consumers act, feel and think about the brand. This is a great example of how the brand manages to capture the market's attention, mainly due to the quality of the product or service. The market reacts positively when quality exceeds brand value expectations. It must be remembered that the industry is influenced by the external environment. For this reason, systems theory is a crucial analysis tool and, for this reason, a similar model was developed, however, with an emphasis on the values added to the brand. Let's see!

Figure 4.4

Brand management theory

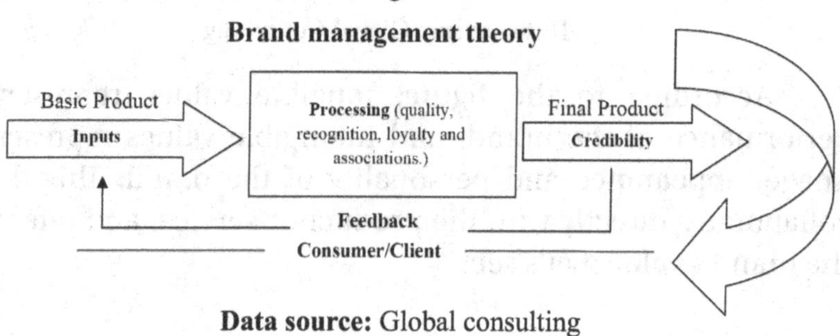

Data source: Global consulting

Looking at the figure, we see that consumer feedback accurately reflects the production and transformation processes of the product or service. However, this same feedback also concerns the values added to the brand. In this way, systems theory effectively collaborates with brand image and positioning. However, it must also be said that from the moment the company has a tangible or durable process, the dimensions of each product are extremely important, in terms of purchase decisions, choice or consumer behavior.

COMMUNICATION WITH THE BRAND

Quality is the best communication!

Communication with the brand is today a powerful tool due to increased competition. Packaging, labeling, brand description, are essential tools and require great attention from graphic artists. *Brand Design* has a fundamental role in communication. Interpreting what the brand represents is not always easy! Designing a communication strategy isn't easy either. The information needs to be useful and relevant to the market. Otherwise, placement will be difficult to perceive or interpret. There are several ways to perceive a brand, whether through transformation processes, price, or even through communication. Whichever strategy is adopted, quality is the backbone of any marketing strategy. Content is more important than communication itself, however, in a competitive, changing and often unfair environment, communication exerts a strong influence on brand image and positioning.

However, it is worth saying that the human element is also a fundamental part of the communication strategy, especially in the service sector. Service quality also becomes an interesting form of communication, because through the quality and performance of the human element, brand perception becomes something more descriptive and competitive. Thus, communication with the brand is adopting measures whose main objective is to capture the recognition and awareness of the brand's value in the consumer's mind. The shine or "stellar mass" of the brand reflects the great positioning, especially in the services sector.

Important tip:

The blind spot concept in the manufacturing industry is extremely important, as the consumer is not part of the final product transformation process. On the other hand, in the service sector, the consumer is an essential part of the service operation and execution process. However, even in the service sector, the blind spot concept is necessary, as the quality of the service also depends on the transformation processes and added value of the final product. Hence the reason for the *stand by* concept in the service sector. Remembering, that we have two types of final product! The end product company, organization, institution... And, obviously, the end product that is delivered to the consumer.

CHAPTER 5

Brand Values and Beliefs

Any brand, product or service needs information and guidance. Which brand to buy? Which product to trust? These questions often go unanswered. A survey conducted in Brazil showed that 42% of respondents have no preference for brands. This index reveals the difficulty of correctly positioning a brand in the consumer's mind. Every minute, this difficulty increases, as there are a large number of brands that are seeking market positioning.

Why, then, do we need to advertise or publicize? Before diving into this question, we need to clear up a very common question. Is brand management a matter for the company? Who is responsible for managing the brand? These issues are extremely important, as it is very common for the company to relegate the brand to the marketing sector or advertising agency. So we cannot confuse brand management with advertising or publicity.

This is a nasty view of *Branding* that is very common among advertisers and marketing professionals. However, we cannot accept this thought as a trivial thought, as marketing is not just about art or creativity. On the contrary! Marketing is science, as it is linked to the formal, theoretical and not necessarily the artistic or creative side. This concept is so true that many brands have disappeared from the market, despite huge investments in advertising and publicity. For this reason, we can say that there is a bifurcation in marketing. Let's see!

Figure 5.1

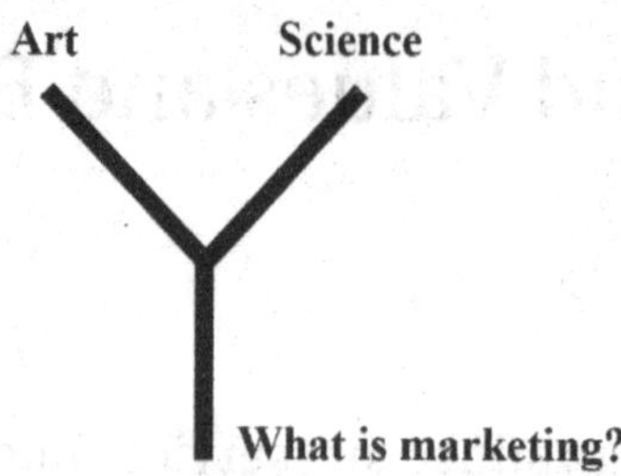

Data source: author's collection

On the other hand, this also means that the brand does not disappear completely. This means that the brand remains ingrained in memory. Given this concept, we came to the conclusion that the brand is a memorable element, however, it cannot survive only with the sense of memory. The brand cannot survive without information and guidance! In this sense, institutional advertising strongly collaborates with the idea that the market also needs transparency, that is, consumer expectations reflect the brand's commitment to offering maximum transparency. Therefore, institutional advertising is by far a crucial strategic tool. Thus, institutional advertising is the means by which the consumer has access to the production and transformation processes of the brand.

It is noteworthy that the brand's values and beliefs start from the moment the brand satisfies the consumer's needs, desires and expectations. In a broad sense, we can say that institutional advertising collaborates with the awareness and transparency of the brand's value. Let's see!

Figure 5.2

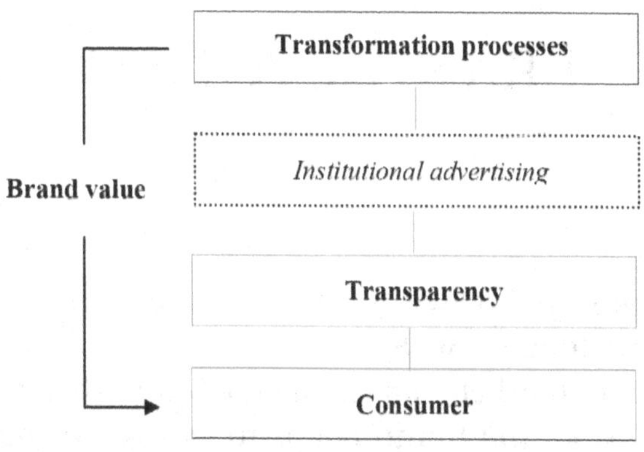

Data source: Global Consulting

Looking closely at the figure, we notice that institutional advertising exerts a strong influence on consumer behavior. In this case, transparency and awareness can lead to the purchase decision and, obviously, to the level of coverage of the brand in the corporate market. It is necessary to remember that the more awareness and transparency, the greater is the added value of the brand, especially in the financial market.

CHAPTER 6

BRAND EVOLUTION

At some point, we must assume that the brand or brand structure no longer meets the needs, desires and expectations of the consumer market, that is, that the brand structure is outdated. For this reason, the brand needs to evolve during the product's life cycle. However, any changes to the brand must be extremely careful, as we are messing with the consumer's mind. It must also be said that brands are not static. In other words, it means that the brand is not immutable. On the contrary! It is changing almost permanently due to the exchange processes with the external environment. In this way, the change in the brand is basically structural and visual, as the change is made directly in the consumer's mind.

Therefore, advertising and publicity are tools constantly used in the media. The consumer is systematically bombarded, and the only defense is to simplify things considerably. Based on this thought, we have once again arrived at the starting point of brand management. After all, is communication the backbone of Branding or not? Despite this, advertising and publicity continue to reach the consumer, and the mind has no choice but to get rid of the excess of communication.

The corporate brand also suffers from over-communication, as most cannot absorb consumer attention. But how is it possible to stay away from communication? The root of this issue can be in the evolution of the brand or more specifically, in the structure or design of the brand. It is based on this issue that the brand needs to evolve and keep away from excessive communication. Let's imagine what it would be like if we could follow the evolution of the brand. However, we realize that the brand belongs to the memory of each era. Thus, we come to the conclusion that the brand reminds us of a feeling of belonging, materialized in the present by the cultural or historical legacy of the corporate brand.

"The brand is like a historical heritage that needs life and vitality, so that it can be remembered and perpetuated by future generations."

In the evolution process, the brand's structure undergoes a new concept in the consumer's mind, thus becoming more imposing in view of the needs, desires and trends of the market. Evolution is a very interesting form of communication, and it takes us back to advertising and publicity. The evolution eliminates the need for communication, as it reflects the brand's current or modernity. Normally, the evolution process always takes us to the end of each epoch or decade. E.g.: 70's, 80's, 90's, 2000, 2010, 2020, 2030 etc. Collaborating perfectly with the idea that the brand belongs to the memory of each era.

On the other hand, the Slogan can also evolve to give rise to a new positioning in the market. Sometimes it is necessary to change the brand's Slogan, as it no longer meets market expectations. Thus, it is very common for the company to realize that the Slogan can no longer represent the brand's aspirations. Unfortunately, few companies really know the influence the Slogan exerts on brand positioning. A classic example is the *Red Bull* brand Slogan. For this reason, the Slogan can never be ignored, especially in the consumer's mind.

Let's now show how the corporate brand slogan influences consumer behavior.

Bombril, "1001 utilities". It is a good example of how the Slogan plays an extremely significant role in consumer purchasing decisions, choice or behavior.

Coca-Cola, "Feel The Taste". It reflects the brand's positioning in relation to market expectations. However, the brand needs to monitor the negative effects of the product. At a press conference, the player, *Cristiano Ronaldo*, replaced the Coca-Cola brand with a mineral water brand. The negative impact was immediate! For this reason, the market needs to reinvent the "soft drink", as it has a negative effect on consumer health in the long run.

However, we came to the conclusion that brand evolution exerts a strong influence on consumer behavior. We know that it is necessary to evolve, however, the help of a professional or specialized company is essential, as evolution involves different aspects of the market. It is necessary to know the product or service well and, therefore, the future expectations of the brand.

Important tip:

The evolution of the motto is extremely important, as each motto or slogan belongs to the memory of each era.

Example!

Huawei: Spirit of freedom!

Xiaomi: The brand of innovation!

Jeep: Spirit of the brand!

Blue Origin: Transforming the future!

Google Android: Moving generations!

Emirates: Excellence in service!

Disney: The brand of entertainment!

Volvo: Different Stories, One Heart!

Caterpillar: Many Stories, One Brand!

BYD: The brand of evolution!

Starlink: The best communication!

Motorola: Daily routine!

Foxhound: Search all on the internet!

JBL: Spirit of sound!

CHAPTER 7

Crisis Management and Brand Revitalization

The crisis begins when the brand fails to meet society's needs, desires and expectations. We can cite, for example, product recall, manufacturing defect, environmental disaster, air accident, economic crisis, etc. So at some point, the brand will face some kind of crisis. The more urgent the reaction of the company, institution, government, the greater the chances of intervention in the consumer market. The company must have a well-designed and executed crisis management plan. Therefore, it is very important to react in an exemplary manner, without sparing efforts and always focusing on the media.

It is not easy to get around a crisis, as mistrust often causes a change in consumer behavior. When it becomes evident that there was in fact a company failure, the belief in the brand will no longer be the same. This means that the brand value will not be the same either. The crisis directly affects the values and beliefs of the potential brand. For this reason, it is essential to react in an exemplary manner, as a lack of reaction can cause an imbalance in the brand's positioning. On the other hand, lack of consumer confidence can compromise the degree of investment in the global market.

In a broad sense, the crisis must be managed with a focus on different products, services and brands. Corruption scandals, bribery, terrorism etc. They can shake any government and bring the country to the brink. Most of the time, the news, in fact, is as important as the crisis itself. In this way, the image of the brand, institution or government is potentially affected. As an example, we can cite the case of the Samsung family *(Samsung's heirs owe billions in taxes).* However, the Samsung brand is known worldwide for quality and reliability and, therefore, it can overcome any obstacle, as it represents a safe haven (anchor) in the consumer's mind.

Brand Revitalization

Any change or new fact can cause changes in consumer behavior. The volatility of products and services is gigantic, especially in the global market. The degree of substitution of products and services is extremely volatile. These facts cause turbulence, imbalance and, therefore, a change in the consumer market. Thus, brand revitalization is a necessary tool throughout the product or service lifecycle.

Revitalize means, reinvigorate the brand. This means that the brand needs to go back to the past, to the starting point. In this sense, communication is the most effective tool. Advertising or publicity can contribute considerably to the revitalization of the brand. Even packaging and labeling can effectively contribute to brand revitalization. Therefore, the company must resort to the means of communication when necessary. Next, we will see the model that shows in practice how this rational, emotional and intangible process works. Let's see!

Figure 7.1

Brand Revitalization

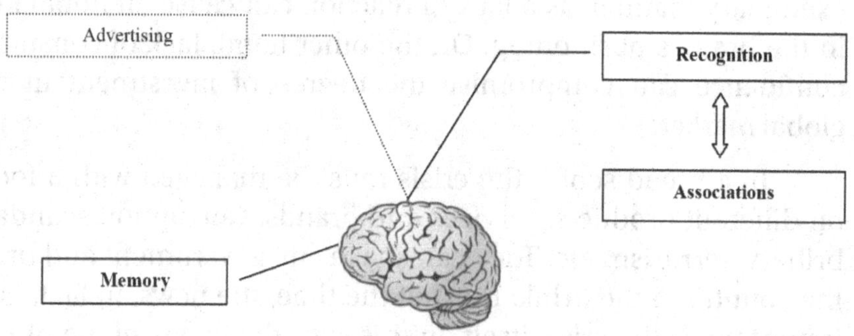

Data source: Global Consulting

Based on the picture, the company needs to go back in time so that advertising or publicity can connect the structures lost in memory. This means that the brand undergoes a new concept in the consumer's mind, as it is no longer just a memory and is once again part of the consumer's daily life. It is necessary back to the roots or essence of the brand. The original advertising, that is, the advertising that gave rise to the positioning, is the central and, obviously, fundamental tool for bringing back the essence of the brand. It is also important to say that memory is always current, as we can recall it at any time. Thus, it is necessary to remember, to connect the structures lost in memory.

"The brand is like an Iceberg, as we can only see a small part, but everything else is immersed in the consumer's mind."

In this way, the brand is just the face of the product or service, but everything else is immersed in the consumer's mind. Normally, the change in brand structure does not bring about a link in mental structures. Revitalization is an inverse process to evolution, whose objective is to go back in time without necessarily modifying the structures or personality of the brand. In this case, we can say that the brand belongs to the memory of each epoch.

Thus, revitalization is a kind of photography, capable of connecting structures lost in memory, even when there are no significant changes in the brand's structure. So revitalization is by far the best tool to bring back the essence and positioning of the brand in the consumer's mind. However, depending on the stage of the product or service lifecycle, it is necessary to reposition the brand in the market. In this case, innovation is an extremely important marketing tool, as the brand belongs to the memory of each era.

CHAPTER 8

BRAND STRATEGIC PLANNING

"The competence of the brand starts from the moment the product or service effectively satisfies the needs, desires and expectations of the consumer market".

Product evolution is a very common factor, however, we cannot forget that brand management is a mental and rational process. In this way, it is not possible to develop a product based only on (new) innovation. If the product has the same characteristics, the market is therefore current. However, if it has different characteristics, it is therefore a new market. Ex: *Blue Origin, Virgin Galactic, SpaceX* etc. In this case, we can say that the market is totally new or unexplored, as it is space tourism where the product, service and market are still in the introduction phase. This market can take years to become a market in growth or equilibrium. And, perhaps, it never has the possibility of becoming a consolidated market because it has very peculiar characteristics.

You need to be very careful about brand overlapping. It is essential to analyze growth opportunities in the market before any marketing action or decision. The company needs to be aware that brand management is a mental process, that is, the company is moving with the consumer's mind and, eventually, with the product or service. The discrepancy, rupture in brand positioning is something quite common in the transformation industry and, often, in an abrupt, harsh way, far from the consumer's reality.

The launch of the new Volkswagen Beetle did not cause a euphoria in the market, despite being a once-impressive product. The old Volkswagen Beetle everyone knows the brand's positioning. However, the new Beetle nobody knows what the positioning of the brand. It is a product with a high market value, especially since it is a once popular brand. For this reason, brand positioning is extremely important, especially from the point of view of the target market. Volkswagen is bringing the electric van, however, the price will determine the success or failure of the product in the target market.

Remember, the Kombi was also an extremely popular product on the market!

Does Volkswagen still remember this?

Positioning, as we'll see in Figure 8.4, is about what's on the consumer's mind, that is, features of the product or service. For this reason, the company must avoid overlapping at all costs, as it usually leads to brand saturation. Remembering that the overlap is not just about the name, but what is on the consumer's mind. On the other hand, the innovation process has a direct influence on consumer behavior. Changes are made directly in the consumer's mind. This justifies the theory that brand management is a mental, rational and emotional process. Branding from a strategic, tactical and operational point of view is an ongoing issue. Therefore, we have developed a management model that includes aspects of general administration. This model, in fact, concerns the strategic, tactical and operational planning of the brand. Therefore, it also reflects aspects of marketing management, however, with a focus on brand positioning. Let's see!

Figure 8.1

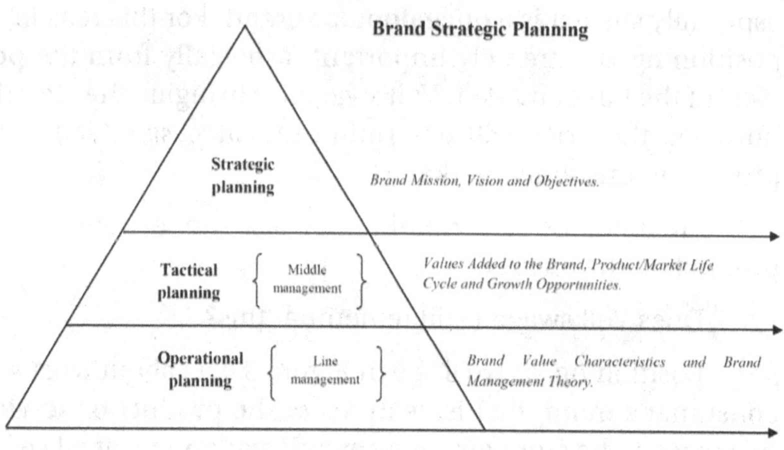

Data source: Global Consulting

Looking closely at this model, we come to the conclusion that brand management is a much more flexible tool than we might imagine. The longevity, sustainability and governance of the brand depend on a sustainable model, which had a greater influence on the overall management. This is because there is a latent demand on the part of academic courses, especially courses in administration, marketing and production engineering, in which the model was initially developed. This model represents a broad and holistic view of brand management, but in practice it also depends on professional expertise. It is necessary to transform this model into knowledge, especially in academia (university). Therefore, this model begins an important step in the corporate market. In the near future, we may be facing a model widely used in administration, marketing and production engineering courses.

Later, we will see why innovation, in addition to exerting a strong influence on consumer behavior, is also responsible for the level of demand. Let's see!

Figure 8.2

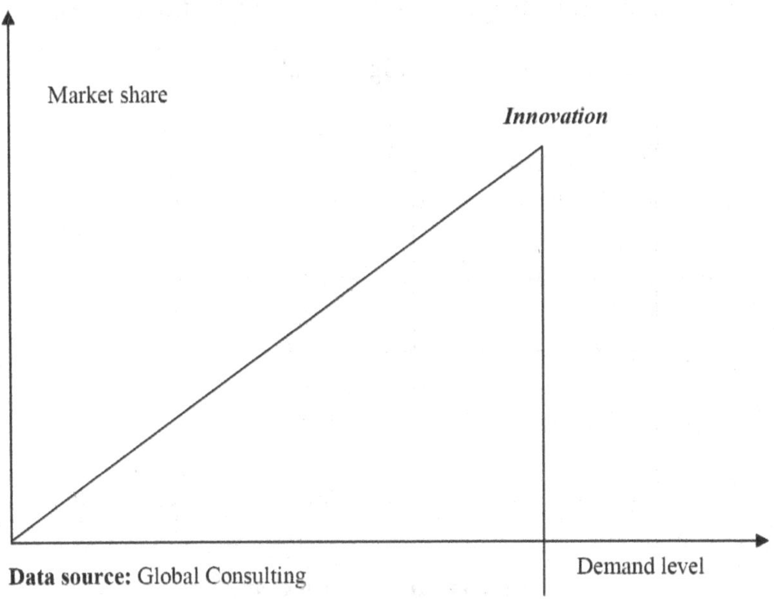

Data source: Global Consulting

According to the figure, we come to the conclusion that innovation causes some evasion and, at the same time, a euphoria in the market. In this sense, brand management is extremely important, as the brand is the only factor capable of putting a brake on the growing proliferation of products and services in the market. However, no brand is irreplaceable! The challenge is to conquer a space in the consumer's mind, and not necessarily a space on the "shelf". Market share is really due to what's on the consumer's mind. The company needs to deliver *value* and *status* to the consumer or customer.

Due to the competitiveness and turmoil of the market, it is necessary to analyze each product with a focus on the needs, desires and expectations of the consumer. But for that we need to classify each product according to the level of market satisfaction. For that, we will use the BCG matrix to classify products and services in different segments. This matrix serves to support the set of products and services of the brand, however, we cannot confuse the BCG matrix with the portfolio analysis. Even though its initial designation is effectively under the brand's scope, this does not only concern the company's corporate portfolio. Let's see!

Figure 8.3

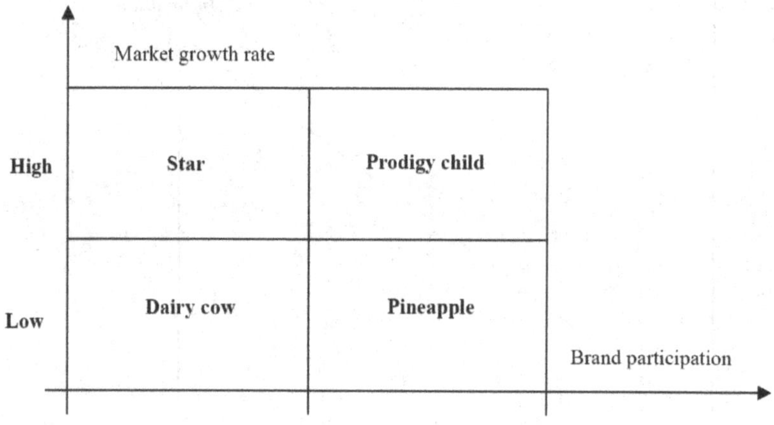

Data source: Global Consulting

Looking at the figure, we have four product levels that are represented, according to the market growth rate and the relative share of the brand. We will show in practice what the matrix represents or can represent in the product's life cycle.

Star: It means that the product has great market acceptance.

Dairy cow: It means that the product has a good share, although with the same market growth rate.

Child prodigy: It means that the product has a certain market potential, that is, the product is in a phase of rapid growth. However, it is necessary to consider some factors such as, for example, lifestyle, fashion, fad or trend.

Pineapple: It means that the product somehow fails to satisfy the needs, desires and expectations of the market. This type of product requires a lot of features that are not normally needed, as the product lags behind consumer expectations.

This matrix has a very close relationship with the product's life cycle and, for this reason, the company should consider the

BCG matrix a fundamental analysis tool in brand positioning. Therefore, the identification process becomes necessary, as the brand reflects the aspirations of the market itself. It is also worth mentioning that the BCG matrix refers to the manufacturing industry and not necessarily the service industry, because of the intangibility and experimental nature of the services.

Now let's show, in practice, why positioning has a direct influence on consumer behavior or purchasing decisions. Let's see!

Figure 8.4

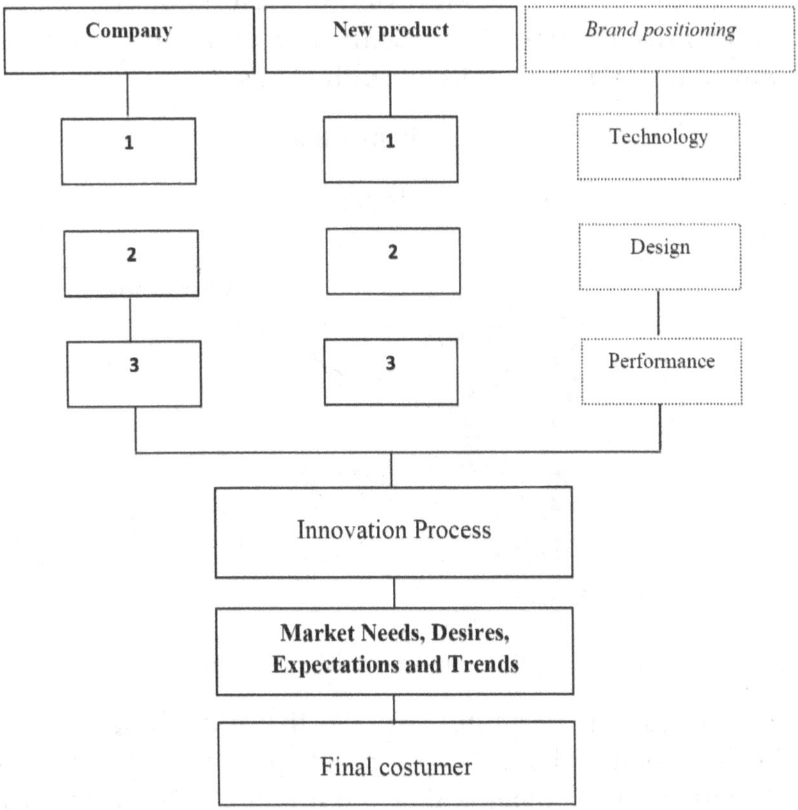

Data source: Global Consulting

Looking closely at the figure, we can see that the identification process is linked to the dimensions of each product (technology, design and performance). Thus, we have companies and products representing different positions. Identification refers to the dimensions of each product, and innovation refers to the new generation or market trend. Remembering that it is necessary to consider technology as an important factor in the product's life cycle. The product has an increasingly shorter lifecycle, depending on the advancement of technology or commercial platform.

The model in question reflects the importance of brand positioning, but in practice it means competitiveness and continuity of the corporate brand. On the other hand, when we think about brands, we can only imagine only nine or ten brands. This in the midst of a whirlwind of existing brands around the world. I wonder why? Because the human mind can only absorb only nine out of ten marks instantly? Let's see!

Figure 8.5

Positioning Puzzle

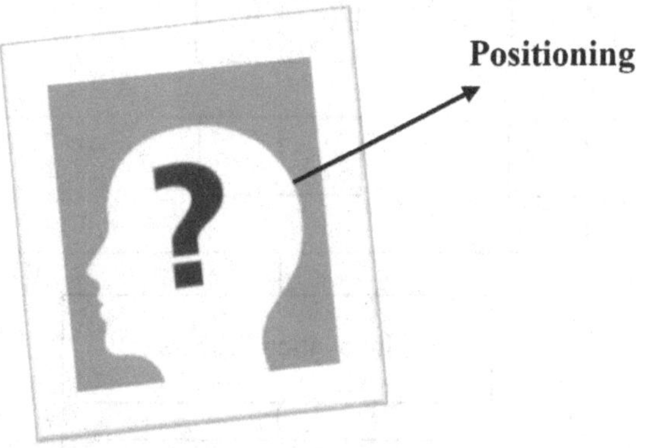

Data source: Global Consulting

Looking at the figure, we notice that something is wrong with the placement. What will it be? Try to figure out what's wrong with placement. Also imagine that the problem may not necessarily lie with placement. Now, imagine whatever product or service is on your mind. How do you see at this product or service? The path of positioning is not necessarily the way you see or look at the product or service, but the way the product or service looks at the consumer or customer. That is to say, the goods industry is not immutable. On the contrary! Today, flexibility is crucial in any transformation process. We can say that the brand is more flexible to the needs, desires and trends of the corporate market.

It is also worth mentioning that the goods industry is increasingly aware of its strategic role in modern society. This means that the goods industry is slowly reacting to the commoditization of products in the market. On the other hand, commoditization is indispensable and also insoluble in practically all market segments, as the consumer cannot get rid of the basic product. Ex: *Absorbent, Prestobarb, Olive, Cream, Napkin, Sweetener, Tablet, Smartphone* etc.

This also means that the basic product has a higher added value than the differentiated product. Thus, the human mind cannot assimilate the differentiated product without the help of the basic product. Ex: **Soda**/Coca-Cola, **Cream**/Nestlé, **Prestobarb**/ Gillette, **Tablet**/Samsung, **Chomebook**/Android, **Hamburguer**/ McDonalds etc. In this way, the basic product works as a kind of anchor, a connection point in the consumer's mind.

However, it must also be said that commoditization can cause some distrust and imbalance in the market. This is because the basic product can be easily tampered with, modified or falsified due to the product's commoditization. Ex: *Gasoline, Alcohol, Diesel, Silicone, Paracetamol, Dipyrone, Whiskey, Vodka, Energetic* etc. This is the main reason why many products are rejected by consumers. It is noteworthy that the commodity school was the first marketing school in the year 1900. And today, it remains a great school, as we still can't get rid of commodities.

Honestly, I don't think we'll ever get rid of commodities!

It is also worth noting that positioning is not just about the appearance or format of the product, but also the personality of the brand. Some brands have bet on positioning, through the appearance or format of the product. The brand personality is present in each product, however, we need to take into account the constant changes in the market. This process requires a greater effort to maintain the brand's personality or identity, especially considering the global market. Reengineering often causes a disruption or discrepancy in brand positioning. It is not possible to develop products with different personalities according to the seasons of the year. This rule does not apply to the consumer who is already with his mind full of so much information.

Important tip:

The market trend is a natural process, however, it is necessary to be aware that the trend dictates rules in the market. Those who don't follow the trend are naturally out of the market.On the other hand, the technology industry needs to find new ways to identify the product or service in the consumer market. Most of the available technologies are actually commodities. A clear example is the consumer goods industry, as many of the products are still commodities. For example: Engines, multimedia centers, braking systems, safety and comfort items, automatic transmissions, sunroofs... This means that we are still far from the reality of what we really should be when it comes to brand commoditization.

CHAPTER 9

THE PRACTICE OF BRANDING ON SOCIAL MEDIA

"Thanks to the internet, consumers all over the world are sharing gestures, words, behavior, music, dance, religion, fashion, gastronomy, family suffering due to congenital diseases, etc. Social media has contributed to an increasingly egalitarian global society. People all over the world are getting closer and closer! In other words, it means a 360 degree view of modern society. So, we can say that the internet has been causing a social movement with a strong economic and cultural trend. The new internet society will establish rules of behavior, lifestyle, preferences, as well as the very concept of cultural globalization. ***The Google Android generation*** *has its own characteristics, peculiar to each country, region or continent. However, this same generation will add in their body language, elements, characteristics and peculiarities of cultural globalization. In the near future, cultural diversity will be a very important marketing tool, given globalization, virtual exchange and the urgent need to present new ways to conquer the consumer market".*

We know that social networks have a huge influence on our daily lives. However, we need to know if the practice of *Branding* is in tune with the tools used in social networks. This question is extremely important and, in this case, we will answer it impartially. With the stratospheric growth, digital communication became part of our daily lives. In this way, the brand became something tangible and flexible at the same time. Communication awakened a sense of ownership, consumption, among groups of young people and influencers from around the world.

It is based on this feeling that social networks have been causing a movement against advertising and publicity, thus becoming a speculative spiral in the consumer market. However, this spiral is also gaining strength among elderly groups around the world. This force is what we might call the social networking effect. Social networks are a social structure and, at the same time, a relevant means of communication for the consumer. But what to do with this social structure? Or rather, what not to do? This question is very important as there is no dividing line or logical sequence between the consumer and social media. In other words, this means that there are no boundaries between communication, the consumer, and social media. Let's see!

Figure 9.1

Digital platform

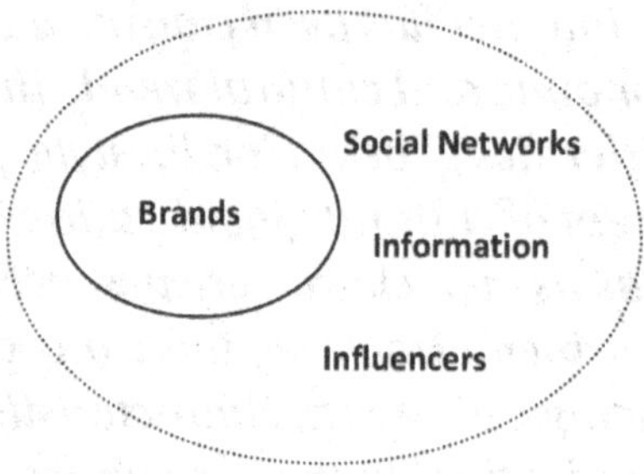

Data source: author's collection

Looking at the figure, we can say to some extent that brands figure among social networks. However, we must finally understand that the brand belongs to the consumer! This concept is so true that brand positioning is directly related to it. Think of brands like *Apple, Sony, LG, Motorola, Xiaomi, Samsung, Lenovo* etc. Now think about what to do with these brands on social media. Inform?

On the other hand, the brand is exposed to the consumer's freedom of expression. However, can we safely say that the consumer is aware of the brand's value? Therefore, it is necessary to make it clear that, although the brand is in the public domain, it cannot be manipulated without the help of a qualified professional.

This is, without a doubt, a future concern of the company with the excess of communication on social networks **(Facebook, Instagram, You Tube, Tik Tok...)**. It is necessary, then, to protect the brand from excessive communication on social networks.

The internet has brought about a digital, commercial revolution, but that does not necessarily mean a commitment to the brand. The fact that the consumer expresses his dissatisfaction or a negative experience with the product or service on social networks has caused some distrust, in addition to an imbalance in the market. So, virtual communication and brand analysis are extremely significant factors. The company must protect its brand, especially when it is in direct contact with the target market. In this way, the company can avoid unwanted manifestations by the consumer or customer. Thus, freedom of expression works as a stabilizer, in which it is necessary to harmonize information so that there is no future unevenness in the brand's positioning.

The fact is that communication is gaining ground and visibility, as the demand for communication services is growing rapidly through technology and the digital platform. The future of the corporate brand lies in quality and in direct, persuasive and effective communication, mainly in relation to social networks.

Important tip:

The more advanced the technology, the stronger the brand's relationship with the consumer or customer. Social media is also the best example of the global relationships and entertainment a brand can offer consumers.

CHAPTER 10

The Practice of Branding in Communication

Contrary to what we imagine, the brand is also an extremely significant form of communication. Let's just describe the topic. Later, this subject needs to be widely publicized and addressed throughout the world. Communication needs to follow the brand's strategic planning concept, that is, create differences. How do you do this? This question, in a way, is a provocation to modern marketing, so let's answer it creatively and at the same time formally.

Some time ago, positioning was something far away, little known in marketing. From the moment that positioning was added to the vocabulary, to the marketing jargon, brand management started to gain special attention from the corporate world. Therefore, positioning has become a crucial analysis tool in an increasingly competitive and fragmented market. However, which tool should we use in the market? We will show several examples of names, brands, advertising and establish a broad discussion on the subject. There are several brand names in the world, but it is necessary to take into account the convergence of the brand and also whether the brand can be replicated in other countries.

Think of the range of names we have on the market, for example *Lamborghini, Ferrari, Porsche, BMW* etc. Now think about what these names mean in the market. Financial status? Which brand has the highest recognition rate in the market? Which brand goes beyond consumer expectations? What is the sentimental value of the brand? This reflects the importance of creating differences in the consumer market. However, the difference is not just in the brand. The mental status is the highlight, as it reflects the physical and psychological structure of the brand. The luxury market, for example, is extremely selective and, therefore, I do not believe it is possible to exceed consumer expectations, just using brand communication.

For this reason, the brand's strategic, tactical and operational planning concerns not only the quality, but also the efficiency and performance of the product. In other words, communication must be part of product performance. The transformation industry has a huge weight in brand communication. Honestly, it is impossible to develop a communication project without the effective participation of the rational, functional and intangible brand process.

Communication can help a lot to consolidate the brand's personality. For this reason, Branding in communication must be used taking into account the male or female gender.

For example!

Is Lamborghini male or female?

Is Loreal Paris male or female?

Is Samsung male or female?

Is Hello kitty male or female?

Is Barbie male or female?

Is Carolina Herrera male or female?

Is Ralph Lauren male or female?

In other words, this means that the communication must focus on the brand's genre and, eventually, on influencers, characters, celebrities or famous artists. This is because communication involves several factors arising from the positioning of the brand, product or service. Samsung has gender? This is an extremely important question, as awareness of brand value means, among other things, that the brand is flexible to product transformation processes. Samsung can perfectly develop a product for both genders, but it can also develop a product with different characteristics for both genders and market segments.

It is necessary to delimit the scope of the brand's strategic, tactical and operational planning. From this moment on, the company can better define the communication guidelines. Communication can consolidate the brand, but we need to know how we can use communication. Think of the totally unusual and out-of-time commercials for *Heineken* beer, but they have a strong influence on the consumer's mind. Heineken beer is recognized worldwide for the color of the bottle (green). However, what really matters is what is inside the bottle, that is, commodities (beer).

Imagine a car with off-road appeal used in everyday life and that does not necessarily refer to the off-road, for example, the *Ford Bronco*. Another classic example is the *Mitsubishi Pajero*, used a lot on a daily basis and, eventually, off-road. Imagine Easter eggs at Christmas and Panettone at Easter. Imagine a commercial for ice cream in winter and flu medicine in summer. Imagine eating gelatin in the morning, pate in the afternoon and cereal at night. It is often necessary to overcome the barrier of brand positioning, especially with regard to specific products or services (market niche).

This concept is extremely important, as the product or service can often reveal more than one identity or personality. For this reason, this chapter does not end the subject, it just starts a broad discussion about the importance of the practice of Branding in communication. Thus, it is necessary to be aware that one cannot play with the consumer's mind, although many believe in this absurd hypothesis. So there are products and services that are merely psychological, that is, they do not actually meet the demands of communication and, therefore, the needs, desires and expectations of the consumer. Using communication just to try to alienate the consumer is simply surreal. This is a very common practice, but it can cause discredit and disruption in the brand's positioning.

It is not possible to deceive the consumer! However, the product or service has to deliver status to the consumer. Thus, it is not possible to create or develop multiple versions of the same product, as there is no room in the consumer's mind to absorb so much advertising or publicity.

"Slicing the product into several versions is to fragment the image and brand positioning in the consumer market."

Smartphone brands, for example, develop a very extensive line of the same product or brand family on the market. It is simply surreal to believe that consumers will absorb an exorbitant amount of information regarding the same family or category of products on the market. Let's see!

Samsung Galaxy family *(models A10, A10s, A11, A20, A20s, A21, A21s, A30, A30s, A31, A50, A51, A70, A71 and A80).*

iphone family *(Pro Max and iphone Air models 17 pro, pro max, 16e, 16 pro, 16 pro max, 16, 16 plus, 15 pro, 15 pro max, 14pro, 14 pro max...).*

Motorola family *(models moto g 5G, moto g9 power, moto g9 play, moto g10, moto g20, moto g30, moto g50 5G, moto g60, moto g60s and moto g100 5G).*

Which consumer can follow an extensive line of products of the same category on the market? How is it possible to hook different positions in the consumer's mind crammed with so much information? Nearby products? Practically neighbors? Regardless of geography, it's virtually impossible to position a product using brand overlay as a sort of anchor in the consumer's mind. Overlapping, of course, will limit the brand's reach and market share. Hence the reason for a highly regarded professional, with knowledge and experience in developing and management brands. However, we can say that this process occurs in general in the manufacturing industry. We can cite as an example, the *Jeep* brand. Let's see!

Jeep/Renegade.

Do we have multiple versions of the same product on the market? Yes! Does the overlap decrease the brand's share in the consumer market? Does the Jeep name represent the product category or trade name of the brand? Is Renegade just the name reason, it has a higher recognition rate than the product's own commercial name (Renegade). In other words, this means that the name Jeep represents a fundamental connection point in the consumer's mind (brand loyalty). We can say that the brand structure goes far beyond the category. It also represents the personality, characteristics, peculiarities and lifestyle of the consumer market. That's the spirit of the Jeep brand! Renegade is just a name! This process, as already mentioned, occurs in general in the transformation industry, however, only the commercial name of the company or product is relevant in the consumer market.

Important tip:

Xiaomi also follows the same strategy as Samsung, Motorola and iPhone of pulverizing the market, creating a kind of barrier to competition. However, brand overlap can limit brand reach due to hyper positioning or brand saturation in the consumer's mind. Example: *Xiaomi* 15t Pro, 15t, 14t, 13 Lite... *Redmi* Note 14 Pro 5g, Note 14 5g, Note 14, 13c 5g... And then there's the *Poco* line, which follows the same line of thinking.

CHAPTER 11

BUILDING BRANDS AND RELATIONSHIPS

We can say that brands are like links connecting needs, desires, expectations and also relationships. A link that is often unbreakable, and which leads us mainly to brand value indicators. Thus, the value indicators contribute to the optimal positioning of the brand, as they relate to the end consumer, thus creating a unique and extremely important atmosphere for the target market. We will cite several examples starting with product recall or more specifically with Recalls.

The years 2014/2015 were definitely the *Recall* years in Brazil and in the world. But, after all, why so many manufacturing errors? The industry is unaware of the brand's values and the end result is, exactly, a vexatious position from the market's point of view. Economic crisis or brand crisis? Brand crisis or relationship crisis? Whatever the outcome, we cannot blame failures on global economic policy alone. The failure is related exactly to the [10]customer relationship policy *(PRC)*. It is necessary to bring people together, manage relationships, inside and outside the organization. It's important to capture the core idea of positioning and turn it into something tangible, not just desirable. I wish the year 2022 to be better than the year 2021. I wish the year 2026 to be better than the year 2025. I wish further growth in 2032. I wish the leadership in 2035 etc. We urgently need to get out of desire and move towards something we can effectively achieve.

Conquest is something we can call human and, eventually, technological. Let's cite the self-service machines as an example.

10 The customer relationship policy reveals the urgent need to develop new concepts, practices and forms of relationship, through architecture, engineering, technology and performance of the brand, product or service.

Have you ever seen someone shake hands with a machine? Say good morning? Good afternoon? Good night? Have you ever seen someone call a machine and ask how your day went? Can we say that customer loyalty is only in technology? Where is customer loyalty? Service? Relationship? Where is the brand recognition? What is our future? Where are we going? Where do we want to go? Will we be replaced by machines in the future? Will it be the end of humanity? Is it the end of brands?

Managing relationships is not like managing technology, as there is no feeling, no sympathy and therefore no way to convert values in the consumer's mind. Perfection is something we have to achieve every day! Quality is something we have to conquer every day! Thus, brand positioning is something we have to conquer every day! This concept begins, in fact, in the production and transformation processes of the brand, which are often imperceptible to the consumer. What about brands like *Ferrari, Porsche, Lamborghini etc?* We don't understand anything about the technology, architecture and engineering of these brands, but we admire them, even without the commitment to acquire them.

Nobody is forced to buy brands! We do this depending on our needs or expectations. This is an opportunity to acquire brands, however, it is up to the transformation industry the role of awakening the desire for the brand. What expectations lead us to brands like: *Blue Origin, Virgin Galactic, SpaceX etc?* No expectations? Is the desire motivated by the human or technological factor? What technology delivers value? What does the human element deliver value? So I ask again! What expectations lead us to acquire brands?

This concept belongs to the manufacturing industry and therefore the service industry. What is the relationship we have with the brands: *Consul, Brastemp, LG, Samsung, Motorola, Sony, Apple, Xiaomi etc?* None? Products that increasingly demand greater interaction with the target audience. What will the refrigerator of the future look like? The microwave of the future? The washing machine of the future? What will the car of the future look like? These questions need answers, but one thing is certain. We need to learn to manage relationships, as the most acquired brands will be those whose relationship is practical, accessible and lasting. This means that the relationship with the brand will definitely fuel any product or service in the consumer market. Let's see!

Figure 11.1

Brand relationship

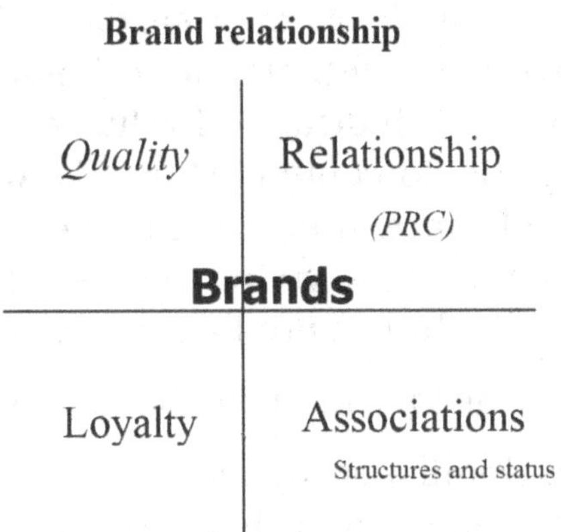

Data source: Global Consulting

Analyzing the figure, we come to the conclusion that quality is the source that fuels the desire for the brand. There is no leadership without quality, without relationships, without loyalty and without associations with the brand. Quality is the first indicator of brand value, so it is the backbone that drives the other indicators.

The brand recognition, in this case, can be replaced by the relationship, because as the quality is perceived, the relationship becomes a fundamental marketing tool in the consumer's daily life. The interaction with the product or service can support this concept. What is the consumer's relationship with the product? What is the consumer's relationship with the service? Therefore, the relationship can say a lot about the brand, especially considering the level of competition in the market.

How does Apple relate to the market? How does Samsung relate to the market? In this way, the relationship can effectively replace brand recognition in the market. Therefore, we are facing an extremely important tool that also concerns the way in which the product or service relates to the consumer market.

We are facing an unimaginable menu of options. Technology, design, performance, durability, relationship, among others, which are options we have on the market. The digital platform is an important supporting role, but still a supporting role. The human factor is still the great protagonist of brands! You have to add an extra dose of sentiment to technology, otherwise loyalty will no longer be an indicator of value, especially in the service sector. No loyalty, no continuity! In this way, the brand will be lost in time and space, wandering in the consumer's mind, that is, without memory or anything that can effectively connect the consumer with the brand, product or service.

Let's imagine for a moment that we are in the year 2050!

A world dominated by technology? Yes! A world without feeling, without emotion, without loyalty, dark and macabre. So how will brands survive? It will be extremely difficult to position a brand in the market. Conquering the mind is something distant, remote, as there are an infinite number of brands trying to conquer the same space instantly. Certainly, there will be no space in the consumer's mind, powered by technology. We are finally faced with the [11]commoditization theory. What do you want to do? How will we survive in an artificial world? A world dominated by commoditization! Humans in the background. Consumers without identity, without preferences, motivated only by the desire for technology. Disposable products! Artificial services! Weather problems! Cloning! Falsification! Imitation! Globalization! Sectoral convergence!

This chapter does not end the matter, it just begins the chaos we will face in the future, dominated by technology and commoditization. Therefore, the relationship with the brand is something extremely important, especially considering the growing advancement of technology. Different human beings, different cultures, different economies, among others, all reflect the

11 This theory reveals the difficulty of correctly positioning a brand in the face of technology and the commoditization of products and services in the consumer market.

importance of the relationship as an indicator of value, facing the new generation motivated by technology. The commoditization theory indicates that we are crawling towards the *Branding of the future*, and that marketing is still a big mystery, after all, when will we free ourselves from the commoditization of products, services and brands?

To answer this question, we've developed a method that can simplify this concept. Called the *QPGR* method, this concept can reduce the commoditization of the brand in the consumer market. Let's see!

Figure 11.2

Method QPGR

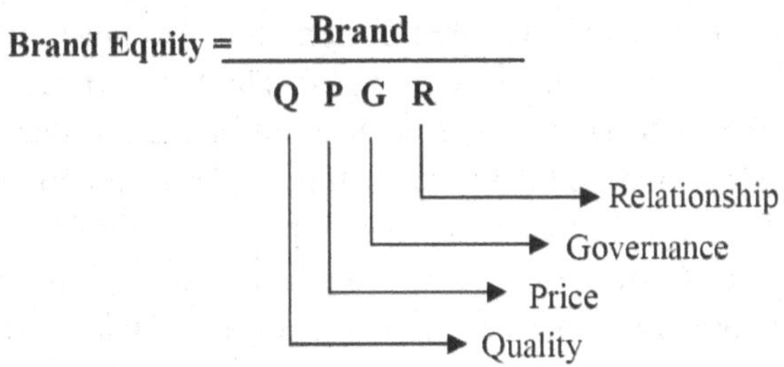

Data source: Global Consulting

This method means that brand equity is about quality, price, governance and relationship. These are fundamental characteristics of any brand. We are faced with a simple method, but which in practice reflects the urgent need for changes in the conduct and management of the brand's positioning. Let's see!

Figure 11.3

Brand Equity = *Samsung* / Q P G R

Data source: Global Consulting

In the example above, we can represent the *Samsung* brand. The brand is about quality, which effectively leads us to price, governance and the brand's relationship with the final consumer. This method should prioritize brand management, quality, as well as the customer relationship policy *(PRC)*. The price, of course, must reflect the expectations of the brand's value in the market. Even in the face of commoditization theory and technology, the relationship will be the precursor to brand positioning. This concept can minimize the impacts of commoditization, mainly considering future generations.

Important Tip:

Sometimes it is necessary to break the brands positioning. As an example, we can mention the Huawei brand. It is a good example of how the brand can compete in other segments, because it has a strong commercial appeal in its visual identity. The Huawei brand is an excellent option for the surfwear segment, such as surfboards, sunglasses, caps, tshirts, shorts, smart watch dedicated to surfing… Exclusive clothing for surfing, nautical equipment, among many other options within the segment. Breaking the brands positioning is necessary mainly because it increases the level of recognition and awareness of the brand, especially in the financial market. Previously, it was an exclusively technology brand, and now we have the opportunity to compete in another segment with a brand recognized worldwide for its tradition and quality. The "Spirit of Freedom" motto reinforces the brand's spirit of freedom as well as its adventurous spirit. It is important to highlight that the "Spirit of Freedom" also holds strong commercial appeal within the Huawei brand's current market segment and the practice of extreme sports. "Freedom that goes beyond the limits".

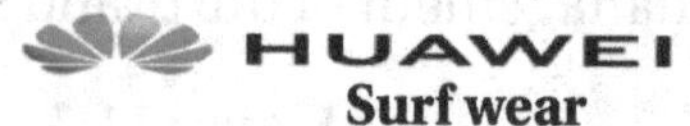

CHAPTER 12

Marketing Before and After Branding

In the past, there was a lot of talk about marketing mix or about the four "Ps" of marketing (price, product, place and promotion). Today marketing has a different connotation due to brand positioning. In this way, the positioning brought to light the importance of brand management in modern society. Thanks to the concept of positioning (Trout and Ries, 2009), today we can evoke the brand image, especially considering the borderless market. Thanks to incorrect positioning, institutions are missing the chance to strengthen their brands. For this reason, Branding is still a fable in the manufacturing and entertainment industry.

With the advent of globalization, brands lost space due to competition. Brands became just names, surnames, symbols, etc. In a sense, we can say that there is no longer any preference for brands in the consumer market. So how did marketing survive without branding? However, what could be an answer to the new marketing is becoming a nightmare. Marketing is gloomy... The market is becoming incredulous, without preferences... In this case, who can we attribute to the lack of trust or credibility of the brand? The old marketing? The new marketing?

Questions that deserve answers, as we cannot remain unbelieving our whole life. Not to mention the fact that advancing technology can make room for brands to compete on an equal footing with traditional brands. Traditional brands like *Ford, Chevrolet, Hyundai, Fiat, Volkswagen, Honda, Yamaha*... They may lose market share to brands like *Google, Apple, Samsung, Microsoft, Xiaomi, Huawei*... Due to the advancement of technology and the commoditization of the brand.

Which brand will be ahead of the future?

Do you have a future or a brand?

Before Branding, could we say that every name would also be a brand?

Today, we can certainly say that every name is also a brand, however, this is a difficult decision, as managing a global brand is an extremely exhausting mission.

If you see the brand as a name, then it's just a name!

However, if you see a name as a brand, then it is also a brand. On the other hand, the brand has a supernatural power, rooted in the human mind, especially when it meets the needs, desires and expectations of the consumer. Therefore, marketing has constantly changed in terms of something more tangible in relation to what can be expected from a great product or service in the consumer market. Technology may well reveal why marketing has radically changed after the concept of brand positioning. Thanks to the father of positioning, *Al Ries*, this concept is widely used by people around the world.

How to compete in a new economic and social scenario?

This is a very important question as we are in an increasingly closer world, that is, the same language and enterprise platform. Let's see!

Figure 12.1

Data source: Global Consulting

Faced with the complex and difficult global macroeconomic system, there is no other option but to imagine what the world would be like if all our needs were satisfied by a single brand in the market. Soon, we came to the conclusion that it would be practically impossible, due to the amount of needs that need to be satisfied. Therefore, competitiveness is something unpredictable as our needs, desires and expectations are being satisfied. This reminds us of the importance of competitiveness and the need to seek new markets. Competitiveness leads us to sectorial convergence, that is, the need to compete in different markets. For this reason, the brand is under our ability to understand, imagine or perceive reality. What matters is how and in what way the brand represents us. Brand representation is something doable and reflects the brand's excellent positioning in the consumer market.

What really matters is the degree of market absorption in relation to brand positioning. Let's try to imagine, for example, what a Smartphone with the *Electrolux* brand would be like. Now let's try to imagine, another competitor brand in the same segment. So, let's imagine what a *General Electric* branded Smartphone would be like. At first, the mind discards, but over time, the brand is able to make the connection in the consumer's mind. This is because the brand is under our ability to perceive reality, given the recognition rate in the global market. For this reason, the brand is a crucial asset, capable of overcoming the time when we are simply spectators in search of strong emotions, feelings and different mental statuses. We can say, with certainty, that this process occurs in a general way in the manufacturing industry.

Wouldn't General Electric and Electrolux be brands of the future?

Wouldn't Blue Origin, SpaceX, Virgin Galactic and Boeing be brands of the future?

This concept takes us back to Branding and its importance in the increasingly fragmented market. Fragmentation leads to brand vulnerability. The economic crisis reflects the urgent need for investments in countries whose demand is growing, mainly due to the international exodus (refugees). On the other hand, the digital platform drastically reduces interaction with the human element mainly due to technology.

There is only one tool capable of surviving a global economic crisis. Quality! Quality is the backbone of the brand's strategic, tactical and operational planning. Peculiar characteristics and value components must be part of this strategic tactical system, but that reflects the commitment of the brand's corporate operating system.

How to compete in times of crisis?

Obviously, it will be impossible to compete with an unlimited number of brands on the market. The portfolio must then be analyzed taking into account the economic crisis and globalization. Non-profit brands must be dispensed with immediately. Portfolio analysis is essential as new competitors emerge in the market. Efficiency is another indisputable factor and the reason why the brand assumes a prominent position and competitive advantage. The consumer market is the backbone of this corporate structure. Therefore, it must be at the top of the pyramid and, eventually, at the operational base of the corporate brand.

Following the line of thought of the global macroeconomic system, we arrive at the preservation of natural resources. Sustainability aims to meet our needs, however, without compromising the future of our planet. Sustainable development depends on how governments deal with economic, political, social and environmental issues. Thus, the adoption of sustainable measures can minimize the impacts caused by future economic development. In this way, we came to the conclusion that preserving is the best alternative. Thus, a series of measures can be adopted in favor of global sustainability. Let's see!

1 Exploitation of plant resources from forests in a controlled manner, ensuring the replanting of forests.

2 Total preservation of green areas not intended for economic exploitation.

3 Actions aimed at encouraging and producing the consumption of organic foods, as they do not harm nature, in addition to being beneficial to health.

4 Exploitation of mineral resources (oil, coal and ores) in a controlled and rationalized manner.

5 Use of clean and renewable energy sources (wind, geothermal and hydraulic) to reduce fossil fuel consumption. This action, in addition to preserving reserves of mineral resources, also aims to reduce air pollution.

6 Recycling of solid waste to reduce the amount of garbage on the ground.

7 Rational consumption of water, avoiding waste. Adoption of measures aimed at reducing pollution, and adequate treatment of water resources, basic sanitation, as well as the depollution of rivers, lakes and oceans.

With these actions, we can certainly minimize the environmental impact on the planet and guarantee the survival of the human species. Thus, sustainability and marketing depend on the preservation of natural resources. On the other hand, we have commoditization in the corporate environment. The flexibility of production and transformation processes makes this process even more difficult. Adapting to changes in the market is not always easy, however, it is extremely necessary. How to harmonize this entire process? Streamlining this entire process requires professional knowledge and expertise, as there are a number of factors inherent to adaptation, including the revitalization of the corporate brand.

How to replace established names in the consumer's mind? Therefore, we realize the difficulty of finding names that can replace what is already anchored in the consumer's mind. However, this decision can lead us to a new position in the market. In this way, it is essential to find new spaces and go beyond the brand's positioning. Thus, it is possible to inaugurate a new category or class of products or services as a form of relaxation of the mind, filled with so much information.

Escaping commoditization will be the new weapon of the 21st century!

NASA was for a long time considered synonymous in the market. Today we have brands like Blue Origin, SpaceX, Virgin Galactic etc. In other words, this means that pioneering does not always exert total control over the market. Competitiveness for new products and services exceeded expectations and the commoditization of the market itself.

How to avoid media saturation?

This question is intriguing but of paramount importance. The premise of any product or service is quality, so quality eliminates the need for advertising. When there is a constant need for advertising, it is because the product or service does not meet the consumer's needs, desires and expectations. Communication is an important tool, but it is not irreplaceable in the consumer's mind.

Modern marketing cannot survive without positioning! We are not talking about names, logos and mottos, but about managing driving the brand's positioning. The level of human efficiency determines the aspects that make the brand a cause for admiration in relation to consumer purchasing power, behavior and choice. Media saturation leads us to exactly this concept. It is necessary to face the challenges that lie ahead, as the technology industry will easily surpass traditional brands, due to the low expectations of the market. In this way, marketing before and after Branding went through several changes, but none of them were as important as brand positioning.

Finally, I think it would be more profitable for brands: Blue Origin, Virgin Galactic and SpaceX instead of exploring space tourism itself, explore the brand's content. Brand convergence is extremely important! Brands with high market value! Technology brands! I think we still have a lot to be done, as we are crawling into the future. These brands represent the future! I think we need to take care of our planet, before definitively conquering space tourism.

Important tip:

The brands Starlink, Blue Origin, Virgin Galactic, and SpaceX are brands with an excellent conversion point in the consumer's mind. The transportation, logistics, communication, technology, tourism, and entertainment segments can add high market value, as these brands represent the segment in which modernity is the connection point between the consumer's needs, desires, and expectations.

CHAPTER 13

GOVERNMENT BRANDING

We live in days of terror, with thousands of people fleeing their countries in search of a more dignified life. Violence takes hold of humanity and contaminates entire nations with particularly ideological thoughts and power projects. So how to develop a productive nation? A better world? We are not going to delve into the topic, but rather start an extremely important marketing tool these days, which makes us think about what life would be like if everything were just an ideological illusion.

Planet Earth is covered by a wide range of brands, institutes, governmental and non-governmental bodies, such as *Greenpeace*. For this reason, we realize the importance of Government Branding in our lives and in the life of our planet. What would our world be like if there were no names, brands, concepts, attitudes? This makes us think how life is prosperous, as institutes and social projects contemplate our universe. [12]*Government Branding* was born here from a fundamentalist ideology, in which people of different nationalities can share the same thought. What would our planet be like without projects aimed at the sustainability?

What would become of thousands of refugees, children, youth and teenagers without the support of institutes, nongovernmental bodies such as *Doctor Without Borders?* We are talking about human life, dignity, improving the quality of life, self-esteem and survival and not just humanitarian aid. This makes us think about the importance of brand management, in addition to institutional trust and credibility. This is the concept that feeds hope for a better, more dignified world, without political and economic interests. *Ex: Israel vs Palestine, Russia vs Ukraine, EUA vs Irã etc...*

12 The term Governmental Branding was born from the importance of institutional and governmental management. This concept prioritizes sustainable development and improving the quality of life and self-esteem of the world population.

The service concept is more resplendent, especially in projects aimed at public health. Hence the importance of Government Branding in the non-profit or philanthropic market. If we were fairer, more human, we wouldn't have a huge number of people looking for a better future in other countries.

This reflects the importance of Government Branding and shows that important brands and names can arise from anywhere on the planet. Brand image will no longer be a key feature of the manufacturing and technology industry. Strong brands will come from everywhere, things, people and humanitarian projects. Therefore, the need to recreate more sustainable resources is crucial. In this way, our planet will have to live with the idea that it is necessary to share knowledge, behavior, habits and customs from different countries, peoples and places. Therefore, the idea of image, positioning and communication is global and not just local. The Greenpeace brand is global as well as local. Global branding concept and local attitude. In this way, sustainability brings to light the idea that without Government Branding it is impossible to survive ideological fundamentalism. Ex: *War and terrorism.*

On the other hand, it is important to remember that just like traditional brands, the Greenpeace brand can compete in the market through brand convergence, partnership or cooperation between brands (Co-branding). The Greenpeace brand reflects the excellent positioning in different market segments, whose humanitarian, adventurous and sustainable factor is very promising. Ex: *Ford Greenpeace SUV! Ford Greenpeace Sport! Ford Greenpeace Coupé!*

Another very important name is located in the extreme south of Argentina and Chile. *Patagonia* is a very suggestive name that can easily make the brand converge in the consumer's mind. A representative name that suggests, among other factors, the importance of sustainability and continuity of our planet. However, Government Branding is even more important as new humanitarian concepts and projects are developed based on improving the quality of life and self-esteem of the world population. Remembering, important names can pop up from anywhere in the world!

CHAPTER 14

VIRTUAL BRAND MANAGEMENT

E-Branding is a term that has come to be used a lot these days. We can say that the term E-Branding aims to manage virtual brands or digital brands. Companies that offer products and services through the digital platform, and this is the only market channel. The advance of technology opens the way for digital brands to emerge, starting the consolidation of the virtual brands market in Brazil and in the world.

Brands like *Amazon, ebay, iTunes, You Tube, AliExpress, Google Pay etc.* Show the power of virtual brands in modern marketing. With rapid growth, E-Branding could become a deadly weapon for years to come. We are not talking about digital marketing, but about image and positioning of virtual brands. And that is the big challenge in the coming years! Build purely virtual images and positioning, using only perception as an instrument of future value. The relationship with the market must be a preponderant factor for E-Branding to be able to overcome all future challenges. The big challenge is, without a doubt, the technology. Technology brands such as *Samsung, Apple, LG, Microsoft, Google, Xiaomi, Huawei* etc. In the near future, they may become brands of great sentimental value, as they dominate the use of technology.

The idea of transforming technologies into solutions is something common in the corporate world, even more taking into account the practicality and security that technology can provide. However, what would technology be if it weren't for the ability to transform something complex into practical solutions? This is the true meaning of E-Branding! Transform technology into names and brands remembered by consumers in the global market. In other words, reduce complexity about the product, service or brand. Hence the importance of brand trust, credibility and governance. Let's see!

Figure 14.1

Quality	Relationship
E-Branding	
Loyalty	Sentimental value (mental status)

Data source: Global Consulting

These are the defining values of E-branding. Quality is the backbone, while relationship is the foundation of that structure. Next comes consumer loyalty and everything the brand can represent (sentimental value). At this point, the intangible aspect is fundamental, as it brings out what makes the brand special and different from the competition. The practicality of the service is, without a doubt, the gateway to corporate brand positioning. Therefore, brand receptiveness is extremely important, especially when it comes to something that is essentially intangible in the consumer's mind. Let's see!

Figure 14.2

Characteristics of the Digital Market

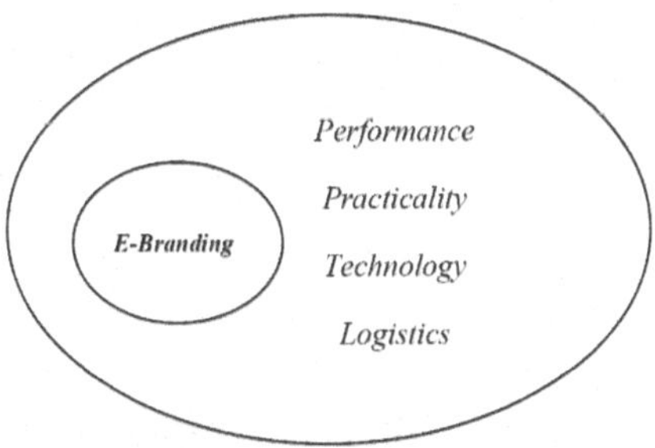

Data source: Global Consulting

In the digital market we have four important characteristics of E-Branding. The systemic process is critical to keeping the company powered virtually speaking, but it reflects the urgent need for tools that make E-Branding a deadly weapon, given the need to reduce financial resources. Therefore, the challenge will be economic and sustainable, given the growing demand for products and services in the digital environment. The quality and performance of the service is extremely important! The practicality and technology of the digital platform are essential! The logistics (on-time delivery) is another extremely impacting factor! In this way, the management of virtual brands is a basic premise and future trend of Branding and modern marketing.

CHAPTER 15

MULTIFUNCTIONAL MARKETING

"Smartphone goes beyond the traditional marketing concept, as it manages to aggregate a wide range of products, services and brands in the same environment."

"In the near future, Smartphones will suppress the traditional concept of the consumer market. This means that the Smartphone will dominate the traditional concept of marketing, as marketing will be reduced to a Smartphone or digital platform."

Multifunctional marketing means getting out of market fragmentation and polarization. Vertical or horizontal marketing has been a hot topic among marketing thinkers for a long time. We can say that lateral marketing is, in practice, a product or service aimed at satisfying two or more needs. According to Kotler and Trias de Bes (2004), lateral marketing is a process that encompasses unreached needs, uses, situations or target audiences.

On the other hand, we can say that the objective of lateral marketing is not to develop a new market, but to find new ways to satisfy needs, desires and expectations. For this reason, the goal of lateral marketing is to find new spaces in the market and then fill those spaces with new ideas, products and services. The objective is to get out of the verticalization or fragmentation of the market. A classic example is the Kinder Egg brand (chocolate and toy).

This is the objective of cross-functional marketing, however, there is a dividing line between satisfying needs, desires and expectations and the value added to the product. Lateral marketing becomes, then, the added value and not a product aimed at satisfying two or more needs. A classic example is the

Smartphone. [13]The multifunctional concept is a characteristic of the market with high added value. Thus, we can say that product value is directly related to cross-functional marketing. However, as two or more needs are satisfied, the chances of success in cross-functional marketing gradually increase. Let's see!

Figure 15.1

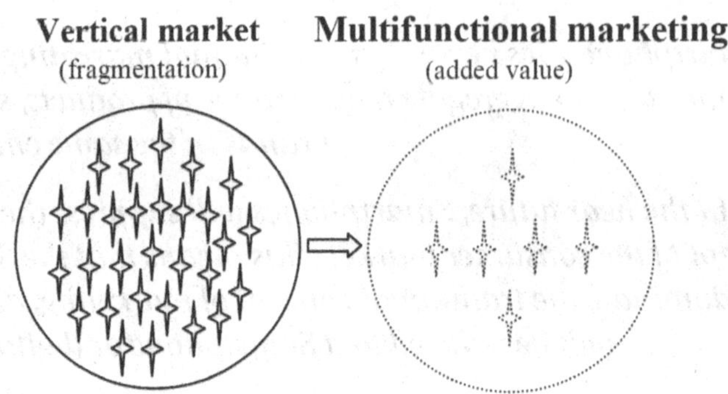

Data source: Global consulting

Looking at the figure, we can see that the greater the added value, the greater the chances of leaving the verticalization or fragmentation of the market. In this case, brand management also exerts a strong influence on consumer behavior. The brand image reflects the consumer's perception of added value. Thus, the greater the level of brand recognition, the greater the chances of success in the horizontal market. It is necessary to inaugurate a new category or concept for the product, and this task is not as simple as it seems, as multifunctional marketing is also about the level of competition in the market.

It should be noted that despite the product inaugurating a new category or concept, it is not free from competition. Any company can effectively compete in the multifunctional market. The image or appearance of the brand is very significant to the consumer, however, this process reflects the perception of the brand's value and not just the value added to the product or service. Additionally, we came to the conclusion that brand

13 Cross-functional marketing is growing rapidly around the world. This concept comprises the way in which human needs are satisfied, mainly due to the added value of the product and the growing advancement of digital technology.

relevance is an important factor in cross-functional marketing. It is important to remember that cross-functional marketing is about a market segment and not a group with specific needs (market niche). However, the market assumes a prominent position as the competition gradually advances. Finally, adding value is not enough. It is necessary to effectively satisfy the needs, desires and expectations of the consumer market.

Important tip:

The space and time of the brand is a very important factor, as space and time can reveal important characteristics such as image, positioning, competitiveness as well as the wear and tear of the brand in the consumer's mind.

CASE STUDY

Why is the service responsible for improving the quality of life and self-esteem of the world population?

The service is a smart way to save lives! There is no intelligent life without human and technological service. Improving quality of life and self-esteem is a matter of government public health. The world population cannot do without a more dignified life, with better mental health, housing, basic sanitation, sustainability, education, security, sport, entertainment and cultural exchange. The face-to-face, human, technological service is the greatest example of the transformation of the human element. Being aware that all of us human beings need to develop our capacity for generosity and humanity is to be aware that service is part of our deepest thinking. We can no longer continue with our eyes closed to the problem of humanity! Civil war, misery, violence, inhumanity, suffering can no longer be part of our thinking. We can no longer accept that millions of people serve as guinea pigs, experiments due to the violence, evil and cruelty of human thought.

Service can save humanity! We can save our thinking through conscience, respect and human dignity. We cannot accept misery and violence as a permanent instrument of thought. We need to take care of our thinking! We need to develop and share humanitarian ideas, concepts and projects. We need to wake up to the grandeur of service! We need to believe in thought transformation. We need to understand that technology is an important tool, but it cannot surpass the power of thought. Everything starts and ends, exactly, with the power of thought! So, we need to understand that only the power of thought can save lives.

"It is important to make clear that the advancement of technology can contribute to the increase in violence, due to the lack of employment. We urgently need to find a connection point between advances in technology, unemployment, hunger, misery and violence".

We need to understand that only service can erase from our memory all forms of violence, evil and cruelty that humanity has suffered throughout its existence. The awareness of the professionalization of human service is something tangible in our minds, as we increasingly need professional services. In this context, the *Human Professional Service* fills an extremely important gap, as it corresponds to the needs, desires and expectations of the world population in relation to a more humane, responsible and technological health service. So, we urgently need to develop a global health program with the objective of helping the world population victim of violence, hunger, misery, unemployment and family suffering due to severe or congenital diseases (genetic defect). Ultimately, we need to wake up to the trap of human thinking and believe definitively that only the generosity and grandeur of service can free us from profound human insanity.

Eugênio Bispo Melo.

Important tip:

The author intends to create a humanitarian project called (Always Here). A global project whose goal is to help children around the world with serious illnesses, severe diseases, congenital diseases, children victims of hunger, poverty and violence, as well as refugees fleeing war and terrorism. We urgently need to implement this project, which is more than humanitarian; it is also a matter of human survival. Let's think together how, through service and care, Always Here, can help people improve their quality of life and self-esteem. Let's together transform the world into a place of love, peace and hope.

ALWAYS HERE, Global Organization for health and humanitarian crisis!

Bibliographic reference:

AAKER, David A. **Criando e administrando marcas de sucesso.** São Paulo: Futura, 1996.

CARAVANTES, Geraldo R.; Panno, Cláudia C.; Kloeckner, Mônica C. **Administração:** Teorias e Processos. São Paulo: Pearson Prentice Hall, 2005.

GRÖNROOS, Christian. **Marketing, gerenciamento e serviços**. 6ª ed. Rio de Janeiro: Campus, 1993.

HOFFMAN, K. Douglas e Bateson, Jonh E. G. **Princípios de marketing de serviços:** Conceitos, Estratégias e Casos. São Paulo: Cengage Learning, 2008.

MELO, Eugênio Bispo. **Gestão de Marketing e branding.** A arte de desenvolver e gerenciar marcas. 2ª ed. Rio de janeiro: Alta books, 2018.

MCDONALD, Malcolm. **Planos de marketing.** 6ª ed. Rio de Janeiro: Elsevier, 2008.

RIES, Al e Trout, Jack. **Posicionamento:** A batalha por sua mente. 1ª ed. São Paulo: M. Books, 2009.

ZARDO, Eduardo Flávio. **Marketing aplicado ao turismo.** São Paulo: Roca, 2003.

KOTLER, Philip. **Marketing para o século XXI.** Como criar, conquistar e dominar mercados. Rio de janeiro: Alta Books 2021.

KOTLER, Philip.; Bloom, Paul N.; Hayes, Thomas. **Marketing de Serviços Profissionais.** 2ª ed. Manole, 2002.

KOTLER, Philip e Pfoertsch, Waldemar. **Gestão de marcas em mercados B2B.** Porto Alegre: Bookman, 2008.

KOTLER, Philip. **Marketing.** ed. compacta. São Paulo: Atlas, 1980.

KOTLER, Philip e Keller, Kevin Lane. **Administração de marketing.** 12. ed. São Paulo: Pearson Prentice Hall, 2006.

KOTLER, Philip e Trias de Bes, Fernando. **Marketing lateral:** uma abordagem revolucionária para criar novas oportunidades em mercados saturados. Rio de Janeiro: Elsevier, 2004.

KOTLER, Philip. **Os 10 pecados mortais do marketing:** causas, sintomas e soluções. Rio de Janeiro: Elsevier, 2004.

KOTLER, Philip. **Marketing para o século XXI**: como criar, conquistar e dominar mercados. Rio de Janeiro: Alta Books, 2021.

www.ingramcontent.com/pod-product-compliance
Lightning Source LLC
LaVergne TN
LVHW031426170726
843492LV00009B/2869

9786501202082